DIRECTOR'S CHOICE
LAMBETH PALACE LIBRARY

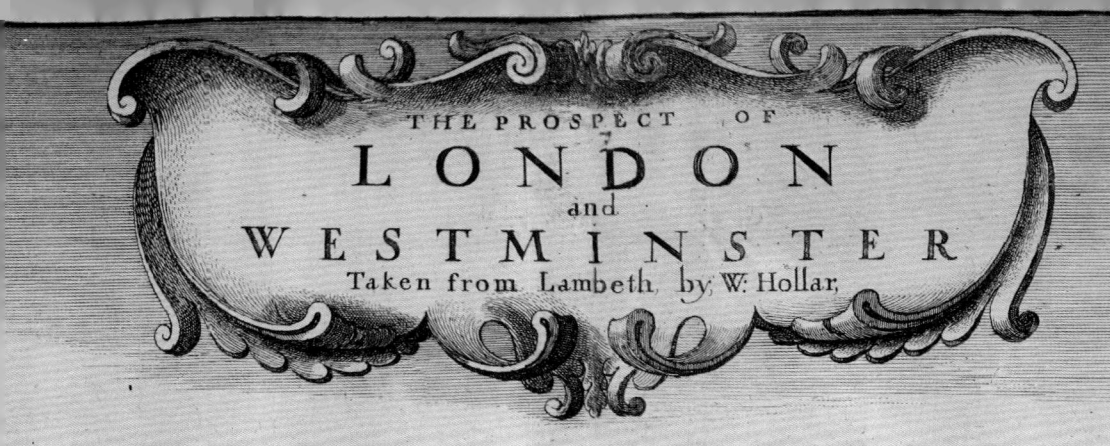

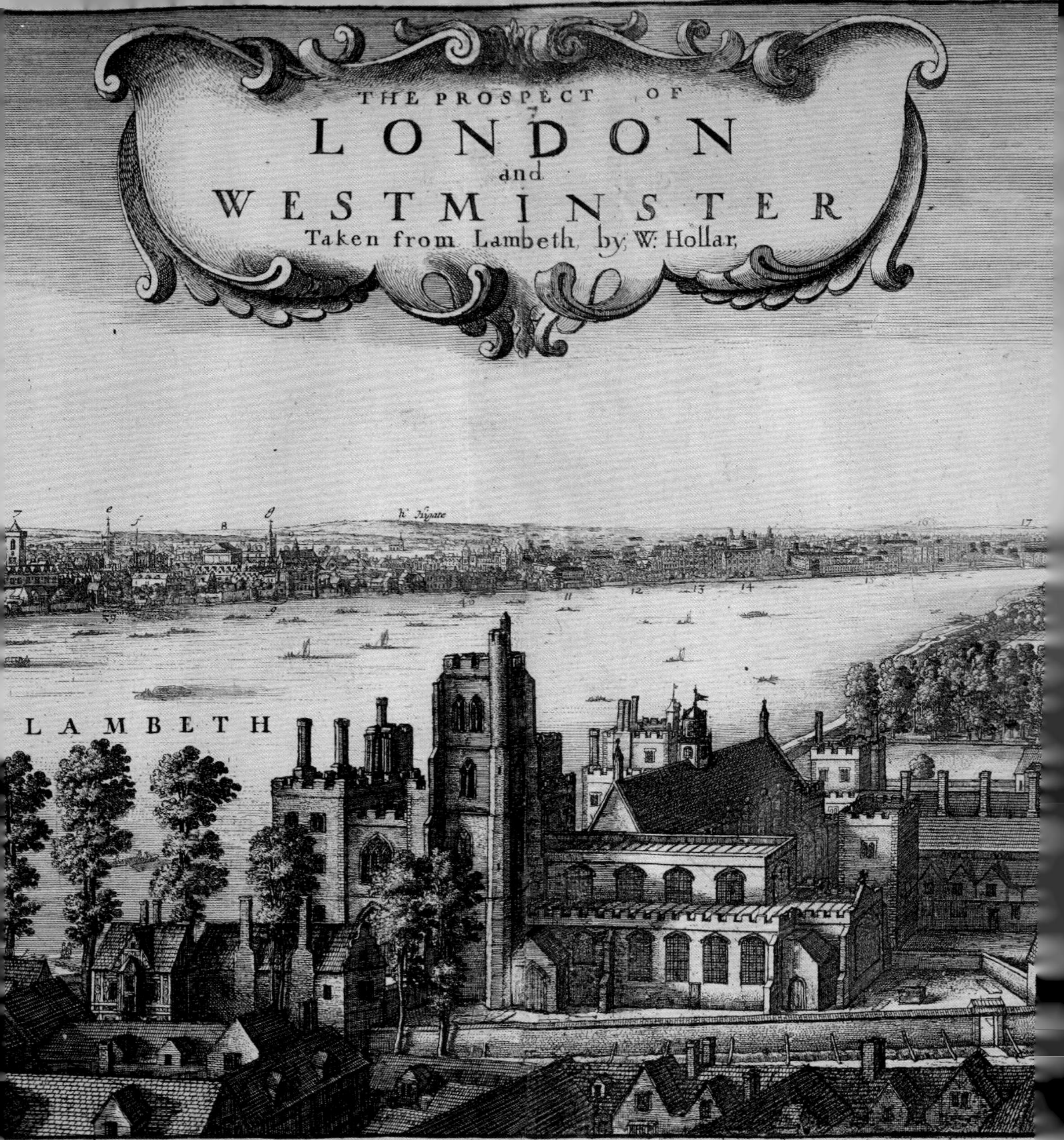

THE PROSPECT OF LONDON and WESTMINSTER
Taken from Lambeth, by W. Hollar.

LAMBETH

| 17 | 18 Essex House, | 19 St Clemens | 20 The Temple, | 21 St Dunstans, | 22 St Brides, | 23 St Andrew. | 24 St Sepulchers, |
| Sommerset, | x St Mildred Bredstreet, | y St Laurence, | z Quéne Hith | ab St Antholins, | ac | ad | ae | af St Botolph Bi |

DIRECTOR'S CHOICE

Giles Mandelbrote

LAMBETH PALACE LIBRARY

SCALA

FOREWORD

Welcome to Lambeth Palace Library! It is my great pleasure to open this window onto our collections, crafted by my predecessor Giles Mandelbrote, whose deep knowledge and passion shine through every page.

Libraries are living organisms, made up of collections, physical and digital spaces, and the people who work and study in them, with their many fields of expertise and interest. I am honoured to have inherited responsibility for these collections from the long line of people who have loved and cared for them since the library's foundation in 1610. If there are ghosts among the pages and papers, they are friendly. With my colleagues – librarians, archivists, conservators and all those who work behind the scenes to ensure the smooth running of our library – we build on their work daily and share it with our readers and visitors. In these pages, you will find some of the 35 or so Lambeth Librarians who have come before, and many more people whose names are lost to us.

Our collections continue to grow. We have recently been fortunate to receive an exquisite Apostles Edition facsimile of the magnificent handcrafted St John's Bible, the 1920s diary of Lily May Knock, who was a servant at Lambeth Palace and the Old Palace at Canterbury, and our first Victorian papier-mâché bindings. We learn more about our existing collections every day, too, as we continue to catalogue them and our readers continue to study them. There are always more stories to uncover, more voices to be heard, more histories to be written.

In 2021, our two great collections – the Church of England Record Centre and the historic library and archive of the Archbishops of Canterbury – were brought together in our fabulous new Lambeth Palace Library building. Co-designed with architects Wright & Wright, the building makes our work with the collections easier and more environmentally sustainable, and offers spaces for more people to enjoy them.

The windows of our new home look out onto the palace gardens and across London, reminding us of the privilege of looking after these collections on behalf of the world, and that of inviting the world into our library. Whether you explore our collections through the window of this wonderful book, online or through our front door in Lambeth, you are warmly welcome.

Pip Willcox
Head of Lambeth Palace Library
April 2025

The entrance hall of Lambeth Palace Library, looking out towards the palace garden

INTRODUCTION

LAMBETH PALACE LIBRARY, one of the few surviving libraries from Shakespeare's London, was founded in 1610. It was established through the bequest of Richard Bancroft (1544–1610), Archbishop of Canterbury, who left some 6,000 books and manuscripts for the use of his successors in office, the senior bishops in the English church. It has remained ever since on the medieval Lambeth Palace site, on the south bank of the Thames facing the Palace of Westminster, thereby escaping the Great Fire of London.

In 2021 the entire library, as well as the Church of England Record Centre, moved into a new purpose-built eight-storey building in the palace garden. This provides much better accommodation for the collections – meeting modern conservation standards and with some 20 km of shelving – as well as improved facilities for events and exhibitions now freely open to the public. Today it is a specialist research library, primarily for the multifaceted history of the Church of England, as well as a very large archive, documenting the Church's national and international role.

Long before Lambeth Palace Library was formally established, there were books, manuscripts and archives on this site. The long series of archbishops' registers (or act-books) begins in 1279. From the eighteenth century onwards, these are supplemented by increasingly voluminous collections of correspondence and papers of individual archbishops, shedding light on a very wide range of topics.

Possibly the most remarkable individual library ever to have been housed at Lambeth was the magnificent collection of manuscripts assembled by Archbishop Matthew Parker (1504–1575). After his death, most of his books followed what was then the traditional pattern for archbishops' personal libraries and were bequeathed to his old college – in this case, Corpus Christi College, Cambridge, where they remain to this day.

The library that Archbishop Richard Bancroft, 'a greate gatherer together of bookes', bequeathed to his successors in 1610 was an amalgam of books and manuscripts that had found their way to Lambeth by accident as well as by design. At their core was the archbishop's polemical arsenal, his collections of the most up-to-date theological, biblical, linguistic and historical scholarship, intended to provide him with ammunition for fighting his religious and political opponents and winning the argument for the hearts and minds of the English people. On the principle of 'know your enemy', this contained not only the publications of his allies, but also a wide selection from the learned presses of the European Catholic Counter-Reformation and from the clandestine presses of English recusants and Puritans. It was principally this material that Bancroft's immediate successor, Archbishop George Abbot (1562–1633), had in mind when he hoped that the library would endure 'to the service of God and his Church, of the Kings, and Common wealth of this Realme, and particularly of the Archbishops of Canterbury'.

This sense that the library at Lambeth had the potential to be an instrument of state power is probably the explanation for the remarkable overlap between Bancroft's library and the royal library – or rather royal libraries, housed across the palaces of Whitehall, Westminster and St James's. Soon after Bancroft's death, the royal librarian, Patrick Young, wrote plaintively that the archbishop had helped himself to some 500 books from the royal library and that many of these had been rebound and stamped with Bancroft's own arms.

Bancroft and Abbot, like their predecessors Matthew Parker and John Whitgift (c.1530–1604), were also keen to take advantage of the unprecedented book-collecting opportunities offered by the dispersal of the monastic libraries. There was a political agenda here – Parker in particular was collecting evidence for the vitality and independence (from Rome) of the English medieval church –

Catalogue, drawn up in 1612, of the books and manuscripts bequeathed by Archbishop Richard Bancroft (LR/F/1)

The Tudor gatehouse, Morton's Tower, with part of the Great Hall and St Mary's parish church in the background, c.1833. Watercolour by Edward Blore (MS 2949)

The Library in the Great Hall of Lambeth Palace, from *The Graphic*, 31 July 1886

but the preservation of the past and the ownership of outstandingly beautiful objects must have appealed too.

While many of the highlights of the collection at Lambeth were acquired at around the time of the library's foundation, other collections reflect the part played by archbishops in the life of the Church and the secular work of government across the centuries. Many derived from activities that the archbishops sought to control – such as Wycliffite Bible translations, which rendered the Latin Vulgate into Middle English, the Marprelate satires, a notorious series of pamphlets attacking the clergy, or witchcraft trials. The archbishops' archives provide the resources for research in depth on aspects such as their policy decisions, their patronage and property, correspondence networks and family relationships.

With the addition of the former collections of the Church of England Record Centre, the archival collections of Lambeth Palace Library have expanded to include many more aspects of the history of the wider church. The property records of the Church Commissioners help to shed light on England's transition from an agricultural economy to an urban and industrial one. The records of the National Society provide insights into the experience of Church of England schools. Architectural historians will benefit not only from the vast archive of church plans and files deriving from the Incorporated Church Building Society, but also from the library, survey files and photographic archive of the Council for the Care of Churches and its successors. The Church of England's role abroad is revealed by the archives of the Council on Foreign Relations, as well as the papers of numerous missionary societies and Anglican religious orders.

The south front of Lambeth Palace, as rebuilt by the architect Edward Blore. Watercolour, c.1833 (MS 2949)

Great libraries, like planets, exert a gravitational pull. Over the four centuries of its existence, Lambeth Palace Library has gathered in a very wide range of books and manuscripts. Among the most important acquisitions of modern times were the pre-1850 collections of Sion College Library, founded in 1629 as a resource for the clergy of the City of London and transferred to Lambeth in 1996. At a single stroke this added some 60,000 manuscripts and early printed books, together with detailed records of benefactors, documenting the close relationship of this library to the early modern citizens of London whom it served. Nowadays the Friends of Lambeth Palace Library continue to provide invaluable support, both by directly funding purchases of rare books and manuscripts and by enabling the library to attract matching grants from elsewhere. It is indeed fortunate that the new library building makes provision for growth.

This book is intended as both a pendant and a supplement to the larger volume published by Scala in 2010, *Lambeth Palace Library: Treasures from the Collection of the Archbishops of Canterbury*, edited by Richard Palmer (my predecessor as Librarian) and Michelle Brown. Using different illustrations, it again includes some of the Library's greatest treasures – how could one leave out the MacDurnan Gospels, the Lambeth Bible or the Lambeth copy of the Gutenberg Bible? But as an unashamedly personal selection, it also draws on my own encounters with the collection in the years between 2010 and 2023, and on some of the books, manuscripts and archival records that made a strong impression on me, either because they were newly acquired, rediscovered or reassessed.

This has been a period of profound change for the library's collections, which saw the recovery in 2011 of some 1,400 early printed books and manuscripts stolen nearly 40 years earlier, the gradual re-emergence of Sion College Library as one of the most important libraries of early modern England, and finally the arrival of the collections of the Church of England Record Centre. Such a huge increase in the size and scope of Lambeth Palace Library has only been possible because of the new building, the first ever to be planned for library use on the Lambeth site. It is to this new building that I must now turn for the first of my choices.

Lambeth Palace Library, London
Wright & Wright Architects
2021

By the beginning of this century, it was generally recognised that Lambeth Palace Library's collections were increasingly jeopardised by their historic lodgings in Lambeth Palace, where they occupied various adapted buildings dating from the fifteenth to the nineteenth century. Other than their charm and associations, all that these buildings had in common was that they had originally been built for functions other than library use and they had all proved over time to be completely unsuitable for preserving archive and library collections. The Church of England Record Centre, housed in a leaky former brewery warehouse in Bermondsey, was similarly at risk.

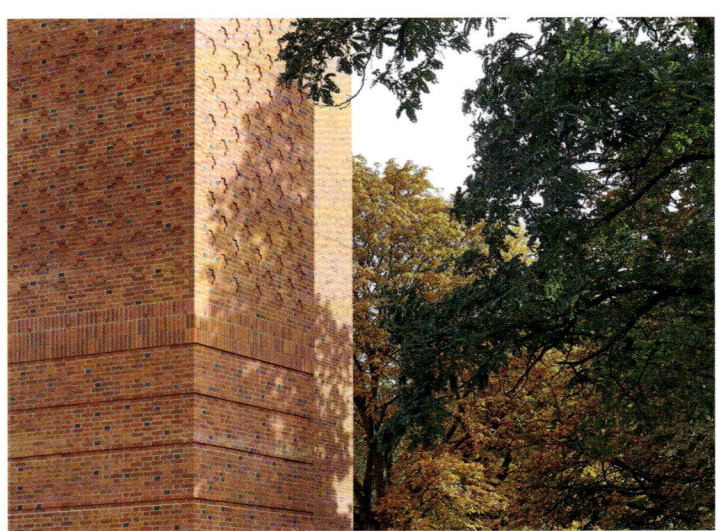

In 2014, the Church Commissioners for England, who own both Lambeth Palace and the library, agreed to support the construction of a new library building. A site was identified in a somewhat neglected corner of the palace garden, and an architectural competition followed, which was won by the London firm of Wright & Wright Architects. After three years of planning and two years of construction under the overall control of the main contractor Knight Harwood, the new building was completed in 2020 and opened in 2021.

The building is ingeniously designed in its relationship to the garden, taking only 3 per cent of its area while shielding it from a busy road. It gives the library easy public access for the first time, with its own entrance for visitors and readers, public exhibition spaces and a room for events and lectures at the top of the building with spectacular views towards Westminster and across south London. There is a spacious and well-lit reading room and a well-equipped conservation studio, but the largest part of the building by far is dedicated to the storage of books, manuscripts and archives. The massive tower, made of thick concrete walls faced with some 300,000 handmade Dorset bricks, contains around 20 km (more than 12 miles) of shelving over six floors, with fire suppression and both passive and active environmental controls. This has provided space for future growth as well as secure accommodation, to the highest modern standards, for the collections formerly held in Lambeth Palace and the Church of England Record Centre.

The MacDurnan Gospels
Ireland, Armagh (?), 9th century
Latin and Old Irish; manuscript on vellum, 158 × 111 mm
MS 1370

AMONG THE OLDEST OF THE MEDIEVAL MANUSCRIPTS now at Lambeth is this beautiful pocket gospel-book, decorated in the intricate 'insular' style of ninth-century Britain and Ireland, with miniatures depicting each of the four Evangelists and margins filled with colourful geometric patterns, tiny animals and intertwined foliage. It was made in Ireland at the time when the flowering of Christian culture there was coming under attack from Viking raids. Written in a calligraphic script, it bears a close resemblance to the Book of Armagh, known to be the work of the scribe Ferdomnach (d. 846), which perhaps suggests that it too was made in the first half of the ninth century, though the stylistic conservatism of Irish book production might allow for a later date. Traditionally, its first owner is thought to have been Maelbright MacDurnan (d. 927), Abbot of Armagh and Raphoe.

As early as the tenth century, this manuscript had already become a high-status object in a royal collection, subsequently donated by King Athelstan of Wessex (d. 939) to the monastery of Christ Church, Canterbury. Following the dissolution of the monasteries at the Reformation, this manuscript, like many from the great libraries of Christ Church and St Augustine's Abbey, Canterbury, found its way into the collection of Matthew Parker, Archbishop of Canterbury from 1559. Parker, whose household at Lambeth included both calligraphers and binders, had the manuscript rebound in an elaborate gold-tooled binding with clasps. Unlike most of Parker's library, this manuscript was not bequeathed to Corpus Christi College, Cambridge, but instead came back to Lambeth in the eighteenth century.

The Lambeth Bible (vol. I: Genesis – Job)
South-east England (possibly made for Faversham Abbey, Kent), *c.*1150
Latin; manuscript on vellum, 518 × 313 mm
MS 3

WEIGHING IN AT 20 KG, the Lambeth Bible makes a statement before it is even opened. Among the finest examples in the UK of Romanesque book illustration, this huge volume is one of the greatest treasures of Lambeth Palace Library, where it has resided since the library's foundation in 1610. The fashion for enormous manuscript bibles stemmed from the eleventh-century reforms of Pope Gregory VII. He asserted the importance of the Bible to religious life by requiring that monks should read passages from it to one another, both in church and at their meals in the refectory.

Very few giant Romanesque bibles have survived from twelfth-century England; in addition to the Lambeth Bible, the most impressive examples are the Winchester Bible (still at Winchester Cathedral) and the Bury Bible, made for the abbey at Bury St Edmunds, which later belonged to Archbishop Matthew Parker and is now at Corpus Christi College, Cambridge. The main illustrations in all three of these bibles were achieved not by monks, but by professional painters, probably secular itinerant craftsmen. The principal artist of the Lambeth Bible is known to have worked also in northern France. Noting the royal imagery and themes of the Lambeth Bible's magnificent illuminations, the manuscripts scholar Christopher de Hamel has very plausibly suggested that it is most likely to have been commissioned by King Stephen himself, part of the patronage he lavished on the abbey of Faversham in Kent, which he founded in 1148 and intended as his mausoleum. To produce a manuscript on this scale would have been a vastly expensive project, requiring about 760 leaves of parchment, with a scribe and artist working in tandem for half a dozen years, but it came to an abrupt end with the king's death in 1154.

The Lambeth Bible is one of two volumes: the second volume (Psalms – Revelation) was recorded in private ownership in Kent in 1538 (the year in which Faversham Abbey was suppressed). It somehow eluded the archbishops, ending up in Maidstone Museum, and now makes a sad contrast to its sister volume. Although the family resemblance is immediately apparent from its bulk and original medieval binding, the Maidstone volume no longer contains any of the large full-page illuminations of biblical scenes that make the Lambeth volume so compelling.

PROPhA

eos compellit ut scribant. Sed uere- lo dei motus. cuncta eoz crimina
or ne illud eis eueniat. qd grece sig- tur prindines q̇; arguens. que dux
nificantius dicit. ut uocent. φατο populi isrl interfect: p eo qd seueri-
λογο̄ρ οἵη hoc est manducans sen- tate uel auctoritate pontificali cor-
tentias. Explicit plog. Incipit pre- riperet ab eo ob impietatem sacri
fatio. legii. Sepultus aut̄ est a populo in
EZehiel sacerdos filius agro maurim: in sepulchro sem &
buzi gentus interra si- &arphaxat. Explicit prefatio.
rara. in typo xp̄i filius
hominis nuncupat: hic
captiuus cu ioachim in babyloniam
ductus. ad concaptiuos pphauit:
corripiens coz offensiones. & re-

The Lambeth Apocalypse (Book of Revelation)
London (?), *c.*1260–67

Latin; manuscript on vellum, 272 × 200 mm
MS 209

THIS REMARKABLE MANUSCRIPT, one of the finest of its type to survive, was made in the 1260s and illustrated by painters working in the French court style, though possibly in London. It was made for a noble female patron, Eleanor de Quincy, Countess of Winchester (d. 1274), who is depicted kneeling before the Virgin and Child. Recorded as part of Archbishop Bancroft's foundation bequest in 1610, the manuscript came from the large and celebrated library of John, Lord Lumley (1534–1609) and had possibly belonged to Archbishop Thomas Cranmer (1489–1556).

The manuscript combines the text of the Book of Revelation, recounting the visions of Saint John on Patmos, with illustrations showing the struggle between good and evil and the Last Judgement. It is not entirely clear why illustrated Apocalypse manuscripts became popular in mid-thirteenth-century England: perhaps it was a response to the precarious nature of medieval life, or more specifically to prophecies that interpreted events such as the Mongol invasions from the East as foreshadowing the end of the world.

The colours of the Lambeth Apocalypse remain bold and vivid to this day, with burnished gold leaf glinting on almost every page. Recent technical analysis has drawn attention to the great variety in the treatment of draperies and facial features, suggesting that the decoration of this superb manuscript was the result of close collaboration between numerous artists.

The Broughton Missal
York (?), early 15th century

Latin; manuscript on vellum, 295 × 200 mm

MS 5066; acquired in 2015, with the assistance of the Friends of Lambeth Palace Library, the Art Fund, the Friends of the National Libraries, the National Heritage Memorial Fund and the B.H. Breslauer Foundation

Most pre-Reformation parish churches and chapels in the Province of York (or the Northern Province, one of the two ecclesiastical provinces making up the Church of England) must have owned at least one York Use missal – a book containing the texts used in the Catholic Mass throughout the year. But surviving examples are now exceptionally rare – much rarer than the corresponding Sarum (Salisbury) Use missals used in the Southern Province. Only 12 York Use missals are now known to survive, ranging in date from the thirteenth to the fifteenth century and with differences in text and decoration. The layout and articulation of the text of the Latin mass reflect local modifications made for liturgical practice at York Minster.

This manuscript, still in its original late-medieval binding, employs two main sizes of gothic script to denote liturgical function, with capitals, rubrics and major feasts picked out in red and music in square notation on four-line red staves. The decoration consists of large illuminated initials in gold, blue and red, with elaborate borders, coloured foliation and other motifs, and extensive penwork. Fifteenth-century inscriptions indicate that, from very early on, the missal was in use in the parish church of All Hallows, Broughton (3 miles north of Preston, Lancashire, in the diocese of York), and it may have been commissioned for this particular church.

Later annotations provide evidence of the cultural impact of the parish church on the local community that it served in the fifteenth and sixteenth centuries. Many transactions, such as gifts to the church, are recorded in detail, documenting the presence in the church of books and liturgical objects, as well as the repair and repainting of statues. This offers an important witness to the religious life of a parish in the north-west of England in the crucially interesting period immediately before and after the Reformation.

The Gutenberg Bible (New Testament only)
[Mainz: Johann Gutenberg, *c*.1455]

Latin; printed text on vellum, 430 × 325 mm

MS 15

THE FIRST BOOK TO BE PRINTED in Western Europe using the new technology of moveable metal type was the Bible printed in Mainz by Johann Gutenberg in about 1455. Although innovative in its method of production, it was also inherently conservative in the design of the letter-forms and in its layout, both of which imitated the appearance of fifteenth-century manuscripts. Space was left for large initials to be added by hand and for hand-painted decoration. Manuscripts continued for some time to set the standard for how books should look: the Gutenberg Bible followed these conventions so successfully that the Lambeth copy was not identified until 1872 and even today is shelf-marked as a manuscript.

This copy was at Lambeth by the early seventeenth century, but there are tantalisingly few clues as to where it had been before then. This is all the more intriguing because it has clearly always been a special copy, one of a small number printed on vellum rather than on paper. Already an extremely expensive *de luxe* copy, it seems to have been acquired for a patron who wanted something different from the work of the Rhineland painters employed by the German book trade. Instead, this copy is decorated with beautiful illumination added in a fifteenth-century English style, strongly suggesting that it reached this country when it was brand new, within a few years of having been printed. It predates, by several centuries, other copies of the Gutenberg Bible that were acquired by English collectors through the antiquarian book trade. This copy might even be the first (surviving) printed book to have reached England, but its original owner still defies identification.

subsecuntur. Similiter et facta bona manifesta sunt: et que aliter se habent abscondi non possunt. ca. vi.

Quicūq; sūt sub iugo serui dūos suos ōim honore dignos arbitrent: ne nomē dūi z doctrina blasphemetur. Qui aūt fideles habent dūos nō ctemnāt quia frēs sūt: sed magis seruiāt qā fideles sūt z dilecti: qā beneficii participes sunt. hec doce z exhortare. Si qs aliter docet: z nō acquiescit sanis sermonibus dūi nīi ihesu cristi. et ei que sedm pietatē ē doctrine: superbus nichil sciens sed langues circa questiones z pugnas verbor: ex quib; oriūtur inuidie ctētiones blasphemie suspiciones male. sflictationes hominū mente corruptorū z q ueritate priuati sūt: existimātiū questū esse pietatē. Est aūt questꝰ magnus: pietas cum sufficientia. Nichil eīi intulim' in hunc mūdū: haut dubiū qā nec auferre qd possum'. habētes aūt alimēta et q'bus tegam': hijs ctēti sum'. Nā q volunt diuites fieri: incidūt i tēptationē z i laqueū dyaboli z desideria multa inutilia et nociua: q mergūt homines i interitū et pditionē. Radix enī ōim malox est cupiditas: quā qdā appetentes errauerūt a fide: z inseruerūt se doloribus multis. Tu aūt o homo dei hec fuge. Sectare vero iusticiā. pietatē. fidē. caritatē. patientiā. māsuetudinem. Certa bonū certamē: apphende uitā eternā: i' quā uocatꝰ es z sessus bonā cōfessionē corā multis testib;. Precipio tibi corā deo q viuificat oīa z cristo ihesu q testimoniū reddidit sub pōcio pylato bonam cōfessionem: ut serues mādatū sine macula irreprehensibile usq; i aduentū dūi nostri ihesu cristi: que suis tēporib; ostendet. z solus potēs rex regū z domin-

Thimoti

antiū: q' solus habet immortalitatē z luce inhabitat inaccessibile: quē null' hoīm vidit sed nec videre potest: cui honor z imperiū sempiternū amen. Diuitib; huiꝰ seculi pcipe nō sublime sapere: neq; sperare in incerto diuitiarū sed i deo viuo q' pstat nobis ōia abūde ad fruēdū: bene agere. diuites fieri i bonis operib;: facile tribuere. cōmunicare: thesaurizare sibi fūdamentū bonū in futur: ut apphendāt veram vitā. O thymothee depositū custodi: deuitas phanas vocū nouitates et opositiones falsi nois sciētie: quā quidā pmittētes circa fidem exciderūt. Gratia tecū amē.

Explicit epla prima ad thymotheum. Incipit argumētū i eplam sedam.

tem thimotheo scribit de exhortatione martirii z oīnis regule veritatis. z qd futurus sit tēporib; nouissimis z de sua passione: scribēs a roma.

Explicit argumētū. Incipit epla seda ad timotheū. ca. i.

Paulus apostol' ihesu cristi p voluntatem dei sedm pmissionem uite q' ē i cristo ihesu. thimotheo carissimo filio: gratia z misericdia z pax a deo patre nro et cristo ihesu dūo nro. Gratias ago deo meo cui seruio a progenitoribus meis in scientia pura: qd sine intmissione habeam tui memoriā in orationibus meis nocte ac die desiderans te videre memor lacrimar tuar: ut gaudio implear. Recordationē accipiēs eiꝰ fidei que ē in te nō ficta q et habitauit primū in auia tua loyde z i matre tua eunice. Certus sū aūt qd et in te. ꝓpter quā causam amoneo te ut resuscites gratiam dei q' est in te p impositione manuū mear. Nō enim dedit nobis de-

Maximus eloquio, ciuis bonus, vrbis amator.
Perniciesq; malis, pfugiuq; bonis.
Qui sexaginta expletis ac trib; annis
Seruicio pressam restituit patriā.

Appolonius Rhetor grecus sm Plutarcū.
Te nempe cicero, e laudo et admiror, sed grecor
fortune me miseret cū videā erudicōr z eloquētiā.
q sola bonor nobis relicta erat, p te romā accessisse.

Presens Marci tulij clarissimū opus. Johannes fust Mogūtinus ciuis, nō atramēto, plumali cāna neq; aerea. Sed arte quadam perpulcra, manu Petri de gernsssem psueri mei feliciter effeci finitum. Anno M. cccc. lxvi. quarta die mensis februarij. &c.

Empt apud ss̄m damiani in oppido bruggensi flandrie p solidos Russel de veror doctorem archidiaconū berkshyrie anno domini milesimo cccc lxseptimo x̄o. calendas Maias.

R͞ni
P Russel

Typographia donū Dei praestantissimū;
Quo Deus extremis temporibʒ nō solùm
Antichristi potentiā evertit, Sed et uni-
versū orbem inexcusabilem reddit. Quia
jam non ex rerū creatarū consideratione,
sed suo ipsius verbo in omnes terrarum
partes, in oēs familias, omniumq; populo-
rū linguas transfuso se patefecit. Joān.
Temporarius chronogr. lib. 1. ad an. 1460.

MARCUS TULLIUS CICERO (106–43 BC)

De officiis ('On Duties')
[Mainz]: Johann Fust and Peter Schoeffer, 4 February 1466
Latin; printed text on vellum, 227 × 173 mm
MS 765

CICERO's *De officiis*, A WORK OF Roman philosophy discussing moral duties and responsibilities, was printed by Johann Fust and Peter Schoeffer in Mainz in 1465. Their edition has a good claim to being the first printed edition not only of Cicero, but of any classical text. It sold so well that Fust and Schoeffer published another edition in February 1466, which was distributed widely.

This is one of two copies of the 1466 Cicero that were both purchased in Bruges, in the cloister of the medieval cathedral of St Donatian on the same day, 17 April 1467, by John Russell (*c.*1430–1494), Archdeacon of Berkshire. Unlike the owner of the Lambeth Gutenberg Bible, Russell seems to have taken great care to record in the books when and where he acquired these products of the newfangled technology.

A canon lawyer and royal administrator, Russell went on to become Bishop of Lincoln, Chancellor of Oxford University and Chancellor of England. He was probably in Bruges in April 1467 as part of a diplomatic mission to the Burgundian court. A scholar whose learning was praised by Thomas More, Russell was also a patron of the printer William Caxton. Surviving books and manuscripts that Russell owned testify to his serious and wide-ranging interests in classical and humanist authors. His two copies of the 1466 Cicero are among the earliest documented purchases by an Englishman of any printed book. The novelty of this experience may explain not only Russell's careful recording of the precise circumstances of his purchase, but also his simultaneous acquisition of both a vellum copy and a paper copy (now at Cambridge University Library) of the same book.

Marcus Fabius Quintilianus (c.AD 35–c.100)

Institutiones oratoriae ('Institutes of Oratory')
Venice: Nicolas Jenson, 21 May 1471
Latin; printed text on paper, folio
SA6649.A2 1471 [**]; acquired in 2018, with the assistance of the Friends of Lambeth Palace Library and the Friends of the National Libraries

Cardinal John Morton, Archbishop of Canterbury from 1486 until his death in 1500, was an ecclesiastical lawyer, Master of the Rolls and Lord Chancellor of England. He was one of Henry VII's closest advisers and simultaneously also Chancellor of both Oxford and Cambridge universities. Morton is remembered as the first patron of Thomas More and of early Tudor dramatists such as Henry Medwall, and as the builder of Morton's Tower, the red-brick gatehouse at Lambeth, as well as palaces at Croydon and Hatfield. He is also the first Archbishop of Canterbury known to have owned printed books as well as manuscripts.

One such book from Morton's library is a copy of *Institutiones oratoriae*, a textbook on the theory and practice of eloquence by the classical Roman rhetorician Quintilian. This work, which quickly established itself in humanist educational circles, may also have had practical uses for Morton, who may have bought it new during one of his diplomatic missions to France, Flanders or Rome in the 1470s and 1480s. Typographically a strikingly beautiful book, it bears Morton's painted arms on its first leaf, and below this a rebus, punning on his name – a barrel, or tun, with the letters MOR.

The volume's subsequent owners shed more light on Morton's circle. William Hone (d. 1522), Fellow of All Souls College, Oxford, became Latin tutor to the future King Henry VIII in 1504. John Cole (d. 1536), another Fellow of All Souls, later became a royal chaplain, canon of Wells and Warden of All Souls. Both these men had close connections with Morton's household and were beneficiaries of his patronage.

TABVLA QVINTILIANI.

CAPITVLA PRIMI LIBRI.

Procemium.
Queadmodum prima elementa tradenda sunt.
Vtrū utilius domi an in scholis erudiantur.
Ad cognoscēdū ingeniū pueroꝝ primum signū est memoria.
Artium fundamentū grāmaticā.
De partibus orationis secūdum Aristotelem & Theodectem.
Declinationes sciendæ a pueris.
Græci carent ablatiuo.
Tres uirtutes in elocutione.
De uetustate.
De cōsuetudine ueteris sermoīs.
De ortographia.
De officio grāmatici & quæ primordia sint dicendi.
An oratori futuro necessaria sit plurium artium scientia.
De musice & eius laudibus.
Cōmodā gæometriā oratori.
De prima ꝓnūciatione & gestus institutione.
An prædicta discenda sit eodem tempore.

CAPITVLA SECVNDI LIBRI

Quando oratori sit tradendus puer.
De moribus & officiis præceptoris.
An protinus præceptore optimo sit utendum.

De primis apud rhetorem exercitationibus.
De lectione oratoꝝ & historicoꝝ apud rhetorem.
Qui primi legendi.
De diuisione.
De ediscendo.
An secundum sui quisq; ingenii docendus sit naturā.
De officio discipulorum.
De utilitate & rōne declamandi.
An artis necessaria cognitio.
Quare ieruditi ingeniosiores uulgo habentur.
Quis modus in arte
Diuisio totius operis.
Quid sit rhetorice: & quis eius finis.
An utilis sit rhetorice.
An rhetorice sit ars.
Generalis diuisio artium: & ex quibus sit rhetorica.
Vtrum plus conferat eloquētiæ: an ars: an natura.
An uirtus sit rhetorica.
Quæ materia eius.s. rhetorices.

CAPITVLA TERTII LIBRI.

De scriptoribus artis rhetoricæ.
Quid initium rhetorices.
Quinq; sunt partes rhetoricæ.
Quæ genera causarum:
Quibus cōtineatur omnis ratio dicendi.
Quid sit status.
Vnde ducat & reus an actor statū faciat.
Quot & qui status.

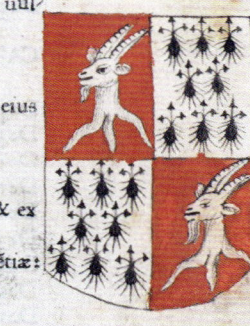

KL enius et domus : et sint mors alienus.

October. Scōr epōr vningy germani sōc.

xviij	A			Sancti leodgarii epi et mrīs
v	b	vi	N	Hac die natī
	c	v	N	erat Richardus Rex Anglie iij
xiij	d	iiij	N	Apud ffoderingay Anno dni
ij	e	iij	N	
	f	ij	N	Sancte fidis virg et mrīs
x	g	Nonas		Scōr maūi marulli et apul' mīn
	A	viij	Id	
xviij	b	vij	Id	Sancti dyonisij rustici mrk.
vij	c	vj	Id	Sō gereonis soc̄ep euī mrk
	d	v	Id	Sō nigasij epi soc̄q̄ eius mrk
xv	e	iiij	Id	
iiij	f	iij	Id	Translatio sō edwardi reg et cf.
	g	ij	Id	Sancti kaliti mrīs
xij	A	Idibus		Sancti wolframi epi et cf.
j	b	xvij	Kl	Novemb. Sō michis in monte tumba
	c	xvj	Kl	
ix	d	xv	Kl	Sancti luce euāg.
	e	xiiij	Kl	
xvij	f	xiij	Kl	
vj	g	xij	Kl	Sctār vndecim milia virg.
	A	xj	Kl	
xiiij	b	x	Kl	Sancti romani epi et cf.
iij	c	ix	Kl	
	d	viij	Kl	Scōr crispini et crispiniani mrk
xj	e	vij	Kl	
	f	vj	Kl	Vigilia
xix	g	v	Kl	Symonis et Jude aplōr
viij	A	iiij	Kl	
	b	iij	Kl	
xvj	c	ij	Kl	Sancti quintini mrīs. Vigilia
v				

Nox het horas xiiij. Dies x.

The Hours of Richard III (Book of Hours including Memorials, Calendar, Hours of the Virgin, Hours of the Cross)
London; *c*.1420, with prayers added for Richard III, *c*.1483–85
Latin; manuscript on vellum, 227 × 173 mm
MS 765

AT FIRST SIGHT this appears to be a fairly unremarkable manuscript, a substantial compilation of prayers with well-executed but relatively modest illustrations, of a sort produced routinely by the London book trade in the early fifteenth century. It may have been made in Paternoster Row in the workshop associated with the illuminator Herman Scheerre (d. *c*.1422). Yet this manuscript has made Lambeth Palace Library a place of pilgrimage for large numbers of visitors interested in rehabilitating the reputation of King Richard III (1452–1485).

What makes this book special is that it has been customised, at a later date, for the personal use of the king. The calendar, which enabled the reader to keep track of saints' days and festivals, has been amended to include Richard's birthday, 2 October 1452, possibly in his own hand. Additional prayers have also been written in, invoking saints of particular significance to Richard and mentioning him by name.

Books of Hours (*Horae*) were books of private devotions for use by the laity. This book would have travelled with the king to Bosworth Field, Leicestershire, for the decisive battle of the Wars of the Roses, and was probably in his tent when he died on the battlefield in 1485. The spoils of battle were awarded to the Stanley family, whose intervention had won the day for Henry Tudor. The book was soon afterwards in the possession of the redoubtable Lady Margaret Beaufort, the mother of Henry VII, who had married Lord Stanley as her fourth husband. It probably remained in the royal library until Archbishop Bancroft's borrowing of numerous royal books and manuscripts for his own use at Lambeth in the early seventeenth century. In 2015, the book accompanied Richard again, when it was used at the service for the reinterment of his body in Leicester Cathedral.

The Arundel Choirbook
Arundel, Sussex; *c.*1525

Latin; manuscript on vellum, 688 × 482 mm

MS 1

The magnificent Arundel Choirbook bears witness to one of the richest periods of English polyphonic choral music, during the early decades of the sixteenth century. It takes its name from Arundel College (the Collegiate Chapel of the Holy Trinity, Arundel, Sussex), originally founded as a chantry in 1344 and dissolved in 1544. The manuscript is thought to have been prepared in about 1525 as a working choirbook for the college, under the Mastership of Edward Higgons (d. 1538), who had previously been a canon of St Stephen's Chapel in the royal palace of Westminster. The scribe may well have been John Higgons, Edward's brother, who is known to have been a singing man at the college.

This is one of only two ecclesiastical English choirbooks to have survived from the reign of Henry VIII: both have connections to the lavish musical life of the royal chapel at Westminster. The Caius Choirbook (now at Gonville and Caius College, Cambridge) was written in the same hand for presentation to St Stephen's. Together, these two manuscripts form the main source for the music of Robert Fayrfax (1464–1521) and of Nicholas Ludford (*c.*1490–1557), who was employed at St Stephen's from the early 1520s.

This enormous volume is laid out in such a way that the singers can follow their own overlapping voice-parts across separate sections of each double-page spread, enabling them all to see their music at the same time. The beginning of each part is marked with elaborate coloured initials, picked out in gold. There are seven masses, four magnificats, seven votive antiphons and one respond, selections from which have been performed at Lambeth on two occasions in the past ten years.

מאימתי

קורין את שמע בערבין משעה שהכהנים נכנסין לוכל בתרומתן עד סוף האשמורה הראשונה דברי רבי אליעזר וחכמים אומרים עד חצות רבן גמליאל אומר עד שיעלה עמוד השחר מעשה ובאו בניו מבית המשתה ואמרו לו לא קרינו את שמע אמר להם אם לא עלה עמוד השחר חייבים אתם לקרות ולא בלבד אמרו אלא כל שאמרו חכמים עד חצות מצותן עד שיעלה עמוד השחר הקטר חלבים ואברים מצותן עד שיעלה עמוד השחר וכל הנאכלין ליום אחד מצותן עד שיעלה עמוד השחר אם כן למה אמרו חכמים עד חצות כדי להרחיק את האדם מן העבירה. מאימתי קורין את שמע בשחרין משיכיר בין תכלת ללבן ר' אליעזר אומר בין תכלת לכרתן וגומרה עם הנץ החמה ר' יהושע אומר עד ג' שעות שכן דרך מלכים לעמוד בשלש שעות הקורא מכאן ואילך לא הפסיד כאדם שהוא קורא בתורה. בית שמאי אומרים בערב כל אדם יטו ויקרו ובבקר יעמודו שנא' ובשכבך ובקומך. ובית הלל אומרים כל אדם קורין כדרכן שנאמר ובלכתך בדרך אם כן למה נאמר בשכבך ובקומך. בשעה שבני אדם שוכבים ובשעה שבני אדם עומדין. כשעבר אמר ר' טרפון אני הייתי בא בדרך והטיתי לקרות כדברי בית שמאי וסכנתי בעצמי מפני הלסטים. אמרו לו כדאי היית לחוב בעצמך שעברת על דברי בית הלל. ארבע אשמורות הוי הלילה דברי רבי אחת ר"נ אומר שלש. לקצר אינו רשאי להאריך. לחתום אינו רשאי שלא לחתום אינו רשאי לחתום. מזכירין יציאת מצרים בלילות. אמר ר' אלעזר בן עזריה הרי אני כבן שבעים שנה ולא זכיתי שתאמר יציאת מצרים בלילות עד שדרשה בן זומא שנא' למען תזכור את יום צאתך מארץ מצרים כל ימי חייך ימי חייך הימים כל ימי חייך הלילות. וחכמים אומרים ימי חייך העולם הזה כל ימי חייך להביא לימות המשיח:

סליק פירקא

מאימתי קורין שמע בערבין כו' אין הכי משנה שהכהנים נכנסין לוכל בתרומתן ותני ר' חייא משנה שדרך בני אדם נכנסין לאכול בלילי פתן ב' בלילי שבת ותני עלה קרבים דברים להיות שרן איתא חמי משעה שהכהנים נכנסין לוכל בתרומתן לוכל בני אדם נכנסין עם כוכבים יומא ה' משעה שדרך שבת שעה ותורה לילא הוא. ואת אמר קריבים דבריהן להיות שרן אמר ר' יוסי יפתר באילו כופרים ודקדקו שמע עד דהוא שבת כמה דשלי לון ומקבר דוחות. הני הקורא קודם לכן לא יצא ידי חובת אם כן לא הקרין אותה בבית הכנסת. אבל ר' יוסי אין הכנסת יכולין אלא אם כן החונה אותה אחר הנבטה. דבר של תורה ר' זעירא בשם רב ירמיה הוא ספר על משום ספק ר' ר' רבי של דבר של תורה ספק אכלה וספק לא אכלה אינו חוזר ומברך ספק התפלל ספק לא התפלל אינו חוזר

Babylonian Talmud
Venice: Daniel Bomberg, *c.*1526–48

Hebrew; printed text on paper, 12 vols, folio

Sion Arc Quarto A70.1/T14B(1), transferred to Lambeth Palace Library, 1996

WITHIN A YEAR OF THE FOUNDATION OF SION COLLEGE LIBRARY in 1629, the biblical scholar John Lightfoot (1602–1675), the founder of modern Hebraic scholarship in England, had moved from his Staffordshire rectory to reside in London, mainly to take advantage of the rapidly expanding collections of Hebrew books that the library offered. Foremost among these new acquisitions was the Sion College Talmud. Issued by Daniel Bomberg (*c.*1483–*c.*1549) in Venice in a series of tractates printed between 1526 and 1548, the Talmud brings together ancient Jewish law, biblical commentary, social history and folklore. It was a landmark in the history of Hebrew printing, but was very soon condemned by the Catholic authorities and most copies were destroyed.

By the early seventeenth century the Talmud had already become a rare and expensive book. This copy, originally in 18 volumes, was imported from Italy by the London bookseller Henry Fetherstone and advertised in 1628 in a printed catalogue, the first sale catalogue of antiquarian books in the history of the English book trade. In the following year it was bought for the newly founded library at Sion College using funds raised by George Walker, rector of the parish of St John the Evangelist, Watling Street, through an appeal to his parishioners. The first volume still contains, rather poignantly, the list of names of the 18 donors who clubbed together what they could afford, ranging from 4 pounds to 10 shillings, to make up the very substantial purchase price of 26 pounds.

THE ENGLISH REFORMATION

HENRY VIII (1491–1547)

Assertio Septem Sacramentorum aduersus Martinum Lutherum ('Defence of the Seven Sacraments against Martin Luther')
London: Richard Pynson, 1523
Latin; printed text on paper, quarto
[ZZ]1521.1

[THOMAS ABELL (1497–1540)]

Invicta Veritas ('Unconquered Truth')
Luneberge [a false place of publication; really printed in Antwerp by Marten de Keyser], 1532
English; printed text on paper, quarto
[ZZ]1532.4.01

TWO BOOKS AT LAMBETH ENCAPSULATE much of the personal history of the English Reformation. As a young king, Henry VIII published a defence of Catholic doctrine against the criticisms of Martin Luther, *Assertio Septem Sacramentorum* (1521), which won for Henry the title 'Defender of the Faith' from a grateful Pope. This copy belonged to none other than Thomas Cranmer, who became Archbishop of Canterbury in 1533, an appointment he largely owed to the patronage of the Boleyn family. By this time Henry had been in fruitless negotiation with the papacy for several years in an attempt to obtain a divorce, in order to marry Anne Boleyn.

The anonymous author of *Invicta Veritas* was Thomas Abell, a chaplain to Henry's first queen, Catherine of Aragon (1485–1536). The truth in question was the validity of the royal marriage, which Abell stoutly defended on the basis of scripture and ecclesiastical law. The copy at Lambeth once belonged to Henry VIII himself: marginal notes in Henry's hand show the king searching for loopholes in the argument. His autograph note ('it is false for [a] son cannot marry the mo[ther] in law') rejects Abell's definitions of consanguinity and affinity, which were crucial to the question of whether Henry's marriage to his brother's widow had been valid in the first place.

Both these books were once in the royal library, but came to Lambeth by very different routes. Shortly after the death of Richard Bancroft in 1610, the royal librarian, Patrick Young, recorded plaintively that the archbishop had appropriated some 500 volumes for his own use. These were never returned and one consequence is

Thomas Cantuarien

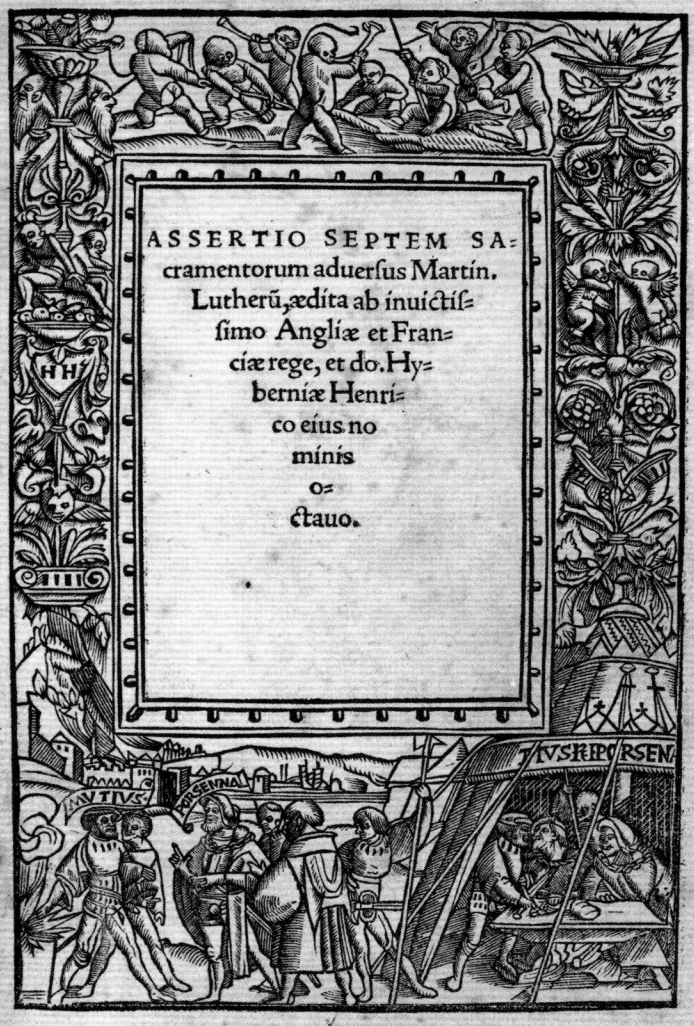

ASSERTIO SEPTEM SA=
cramentorum aduersus Martin.
Lutherũ, ædita ab inuictis=
simo Angliæ et Fran
ciæ rege, et do. Hy
berniæ Henri=
co eius no
minis
o=
ctauo.

Lumley

INVICTA VERITAS.

An answere, That by no maner of lawe, it maye be lawfull for the moste noble kinge of englande, kinge Henry the ayght to be diuorsed fro the quenes grace, his lawful and very wyfe.

Sette a parte Cristen reader all blynde affeccion: and read this boke with iugement, conferringe it with the tother boke agenst which this is writen: and I doute not, but thou shalt stande on the quenis parte, as a fauourer of the firme and inuincible Verite.

BIBLIOTHECA LAMBETHANA

that Lambeth Palace Library now preserves more of the scattered books and manuscripts from the library of Henry VIII than any other institution apart from the British Library. Cranmer's copy of the *Assertio*, by contrast, passed into the collections of the British Museum and was unceremoniously sold off as a duplicate in 1769. It was eventually bought by the American millionaire collector J.P. Morgan Jr, who thought it a suitable Christmas present in 1938 for Archbishop Cosmo Gordon Lang (1864–1945).

THE ENGLISH COUNTER-REFORMATION

Prayers or collectes to be sayd in the Masse for the Quenes highnesse, beinge with childe
London: John Cawood [1554?]
English and Latin; printed text on paper, 258 x 171 mm
H2015.S2 02 [**], presented through the Friends of Lambeth Palace Library, 2014

Register of Cardinal Reginald Pole
London, 1556–58
Latin; manuscript on parchment, 420 x 345 mm
Reg. Pole

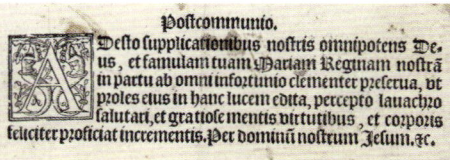

THESE TWO DOCUMENTS LINK two key figures in the English Counter-Reformation, Queen Mary I (1516–1558) and her cousin Reginald Pole (1500–1558), Cardinal and Archbishop of Canterbury. A remarkable and unique survival, which entered the Lambeth collections in 2014, is a single leaf containing Latin prayers for Mary Tudor. This was printed by the Queen's Printer, John Cawood, at a time when it was wrongly believed that the queen was pregnant, following her marriage to Philip of Spain. In late November 1554 a celebratory mass, with a public procession, was held at St Paul's Cathedral. Presumably the prayers were printed and circulated for this occasion, as hopes rose for the continuity of the Roman Catholic succession.

It was at this moment that Reginald Pole returned to England as papal legate, charged with reconciling England to the authority of Rome. He had spent the previous 20 years in European exile, caught up in the turbulent politics and diplomacy of the papacy and Holy Roman Empire and very narrowly missing election himself as Pope in 1549. Pole became Archbishop formally in March 1556, a few days after the execution of Thomas Cranmer. His register forms part of the long series of archiepiscopal registers at Lambeth that runs from 1279 to 1928 in an almost unbroken sequence. This volume, the last for a Roman Catholic archbishop, opens with Pole's elaborate and splendidly painted personal coat of arms, incorporating the royal arms of England, positioned between his cardinal's hat and the arms of the see of Canterbury. It is a record of intense activity cut short, for by coincidence he and Mary both died on the same day, 17 November 1558.

Sir Thomas North (1535–1603?)

The Jorney of the Queenes Ambassadours unto Roome Anno 1555
*c.*1555–59; possibly autograph
English; manuscript on paper, 310 × 205 mm
MS 5076; acquired in 2015, with the assistance of the Friends of Lambeth Palace Library, the Friends of the National Libraries and the Arts Council England/V&A Purchase Grant Fund

Thomas Thirlby (*c.*1500–1570), Bishop of Ely, was one of the last generation of Tudor bishops who were also diplomats in the service of the state. In 1555 he was sent off on a mission to gain papal confirmation for Cardinal Pole's plans to reunite the English church with Rome. Arriving in Rome after three months on the road, he found a newly elected and pro-French Pope, Paul IV (1476–1559). Despite this awkwardness, the negotiations were completed successfully.

The author of this lively eyewitness account of Thirlby's travels has recently been identified as Thomas North, then aged only 20 and working as Thirlby's secretary. In France, North describes the royal regalia in the church of St Denis, an astronomical instrument designed by Oronce Finé and the newly built château and gardens of Écouen. In Italy, they dined in the great charterhouse of Pavia, observed marriage customs in Milan, admired the fine jewels worn at the ducal court of Mantua and saw a Jewish market on a Sunday, as well as a giant tortoise, in Ferrara. In Rome itself, where they remained for 14 days, the journal has much to say about the papal court and the processions, ceremonies and costumes of the Roman clergy, though North's attitude to relics and superstitious rituals remained sceptical.

Following the accession of Elizabeth I, the paths of Thirlby and North diverged. Thirlby refused to swear the oath of supremacy in 1559 and spent the last seven years of his life under house arrest at Lambeth Palace. North's profoundly influential translation (from French) of Plutarch's *The Lives of the Noble Grecians and Romanes* was published in 1579, with a dedication to the queen.

June

[left page, partial - left margin cut off]

...berge of Julius Cesar. (as in William...
...ster description of Italye ye may...
...mes, or Bathes.)

...ter Popes, Julius Tertius, and Mar...
...lus) had made greate provision for...
...ch of S. Marke: he nothinge preju...
...d Pope, Paulus Quartus, did...
...ses. The eight daye at nighte...
...for, and sodden great weakenes...
...m suffered to rem into the chamber.
...n the morninge Cardynall Caraffa
...e presently made rayd place on ye 7.
...ch the presentes 3 barelles 3...
...eses, 10. Romane cheeses made in Rome
...pons and pikins, 52. spades of
...nges of virgin wyne, 24. lb of
...irgin waxe: 10. suger loves, vj
...yne, and 50. quarters of pheasly...
...se.

...he went to the Conclave accompanied
...bisshopps, nobles men, and gentlemen
...o every ordinance. As they passed
...S. Angelo, the ℞ were saluted w/
...ordinance.

A (or consistorie)

...n the Conclave when it was ope...
...taking a heavy verye respe...
...of a wonderfull prayer upon...
...place where he sate was wayted...
...might not come in to troble the...
...e Cardynale sate upon benches w/...
...onde about the Popes holynes, the
...underneath them, and the Popes footmen
...de. After my L. my m...

---

the Bysshoppe of Ely had ended his oration made to the
Pope, they all the tyme kneeleinge of the ℞. Evryone was
called for, and kneeleinge before the Pope to kysse the
Popes holynes foote, who hadde a redd slipper on, that
had a crosse of silver sette upon it. That done, the Pope
blessed us and so we departed pontified.

The 11. daye the ℞. visited divers of the Cardynalls, and
at the Cardynall of Pisa his howse I saw a lyve Ostrich
and plucked a whole feather from it.

A lyve Ostriche

The 12. daye, in the morninge the ℞. heard a dirge masse
at the Spanishe churche for the Emperours mother,
where we hadde every one of us a taper geven us
to holde the masse tyme in o. handes. That daye the
℞. dyned w/ Cardynall Caraffa at a place called
Bel videre, a towre to saye, to faire to look on: so called
for that it standeth in purye a very good ayre, and hath
the most pleasant prospect of all the pillares to Rome:
After dynner the ℞. went to visit other Cardynalls w/ lodge in the Popes Courte: and so went the
℞. to the chamber of presence to waite upon the Pope
who they came first into that came out to recevinge. When they came first into
the presence, they founde but one Cardynall there.
So very soddonly salutinge and then afterwardes
there came 2. of the Cardynalls together, and some tyme
3. and so came in still till they made the number
of 30. And when as they came over the bridge of
S. Angelo, whether it were one. 2. or 3. Cardynalls together,
so many as they were so many peeces of ordinance were
shott out of the Castelle for any honor that the Pope is bounde
so to observe to the weltbeloved brethren, w/ serveth they
passe the bridge what they come to the Courte or no. That
done all the Cardynalles d came to the latter gate of the
Popes pallace, and comme in hise doo up the narrowing
stayer comminge. When suche ten sowre after all the
Cardynalls were come into the presence chamber, they came
the Popes holynes out of the privie chamber amonge
them: they all risinge up at the sight of him. below they

A STOLEN HOARD RETURNED

ROBERT ADAMS (d. 1595)

Expeditionis Hispanorum in Angliam vera descriptio. Anno Do: M D LXXXVIII ('A true description of the Spanish assault on England, 1588')
London: Augustine Ryther [1590?]
English; printed text on paper, folio
KA360.A3 01 [**]

IN FEBRUARY 2011, A LETTER arrived at Lambeth from a firm of solicitors. Their client, as the letter explained, had worked briefly at the library more than 35 years earlier. On his deathbed, he had left instructions for the solicitors to make contact regarding some library property that might be found at his home. This came as a complete surprise. But the library's files revealed that in 1975 it had been the victim of an unsolved theft of some important early printed books. They were stolen so many years ago that all hope of ever getting them back had long since been abandoned and even the memory of them had faded.

When the books were returned later in 2011 – some 1,400 titles in all – they significantly broadened the profile of the library's early collections. A large proportion had belonged to Archbishops Whitgift, Bancroft and Abbot, the library's founders. In particular, the archbishops' lively interest in the voyages of exploration being undertaken by their contemporaries, and in the discovery and mapping of new worlds, had been obscured by the systematic removal of books on travel, cosmography and navigation. These included some splendid coloured atlases and some of the most visually spectacular illustrated books.

One example is this volume, which contains ten coloured engravings charting the English victory over the Spanish Armada in 1588. The Armada is shown under attack in the English Channel and at various stages in its ill-fated voyage around the British Isles. Dedicated to the English admiral Lord Howard of Effingham, they were drawn by Robert Adams, surveyor of the Queen's buildings, and form an important visual record of these events.

AN AGE OF CONTROVERSY

[JOHN PENRY (1563–1593)]

A briefe discouery of the vntruthes and slanders contained in a sermon preached the 8 Februarie 1588 by D. Bancroft
[Edinburgh: Robert Waldegrave, 1590]
English; printed text on paper, quarto
[ZZ]1588.11.01

[HENRY JACOB (1563–1624)]

To the right high and mightie Prince, Iames ... King of Great Britannie,... an humble supplication for toleration and libertie
[Middelburg: Richard Schilders], 1609
English; printed text on paper, quarto
[ZZ]1609.42

THE EARLY PRINTED COLLECTIONS at Lambeth Palace Library were formed at a time when the English church establishment was fighting a war on two fronts, caught between the Catholic Counter-Reformation and those English Protestants who favoured more radical reform, especially of church organisation and government. Two short pamphlets from the foundation bequest of Archbishop Richard Bancroft exemplify the bitterness of the disputes between fellow Protestants.

Years before Bancroft was himself appointed as a bishop, he preached an explosive sermon that vehemently attacked the Puritans, asserting the authority of bishops and defending the institution of episcopacy. It quickly found its way into print, but it was also reprinted (anonymously) by one of Bancroft's opponents, John Penry, in a format that combined short passages from the original sermon with many pages of closely argued refutation. The margins and interleaved pages of Bancroft's own copy of *A briefe discouery of the vntruthes and slanders contained in a sermon preached the 8 Februarie 1588* are filled with Bancroft's handwriting, mounting an indignant self-defence and vigorous counter-attack.

In 1609, another Puritan controversialist, Henry Jacob, published an open letter to James I (1566–1625), appealing for toleration in matters of church governance. The copy now at Lambeth was read by none other than the king himself and contains his furious retorts, written in the margins in his own hand. It was sent on to Bancroft, then Archbishop of Canterbury, perhaps to make it absolutely clear that toleration had no place on the king's agenda.

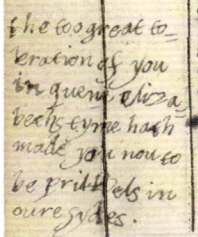

48   LAMBETH PALACE LIBRARY

ſo act. 12. 47.

116

D. BANCROFT page 6. line 13.

VVhere this ecclesiasticall Synod is not erected, they say Gods ordinance is not performed: the office of Christ as he is a King, is not acknowledged: in effect, with out this gouernement, we can neuer attaine to a right and trewe feeling, of christian religion, but are to be reckoned among those, who say of Christ; we wil not haue this man to raigne ouer vs.

Luke. 19. 27.

ANSVVERE.

As though we desire ecclesiastical Synods, to be erected in euery congregation, and parish, or that we make no difference, betwene a Synod, which is a meeting of al the ministers, and elders, if occasion should require, (or more properly of some choise ministers and elders) in a whole prouince, or more generall, and the Eldershippe: which containeth the gouernors, to wit the Pastors Doctors and elders of one only congregation. The reader may se what a meet man you are to be an inueigher against the eldership, whereas you knowe not what it meaneth, and whether a Synod and an Eldership be al one or not.

Where this forme of ecclesiastical gouernement is not erected there, indeed we say, that Gods ordinance concerning the regiment of his church is not wholy obserued: but that his whole ordinance is wanting, where there is a faythful teacher we neuer as yet affirmed. And therefore if by your generall speach (that wee say Gods ordinance is not performed &c.) you meane that we denye any part thereof, to be, where the gouernement by the Eldership is not established, you doe but followe your owne humor, that is beare false witnesse against the truth, and those that professe the same.

The office of Christ as he is a King, is boath to teach

I call it a Synod in a larger signification: yet the worde ſtrictly taken as ſayd ere now is called a committy of Synods Classicall.

But wheare is there a faythfull teacher?

THE
Second part of Henrie
the fourth, continuing to his death,
and coronation of Henrie
the fift.

With the humours of sir Iohn Fal-
staffe, and swaggering
Pistoll.

As it hath been sundrie times publikely
acted by the right honourable, the Lord
Chamberlaine his seruants.

Written by William Shakespeare.

LONDON
Printed by V.S. for Andrew Wise, and
William Aspley.
1600.

WILLIAM SHAKESPEARE (1564–1616)

The Second part of Henrie the fourth
London: V[alentine]. S[immes]. for Andrew Wise and
William Aspley, 1600
English; printed text on paper, quarto
1600.22.06

In August 1600, at a time of heightened political tension, the booksellers Andrew Wise and William Aspley registered at Stationers' Hall their interest in the second part of Henry IV 'by master Shakespere'. This copy of the printed play is bound in a contemporary parchment wrapper with five other literary and historical works, all published in 1600, which bear witness to Richard Bancroft's participation in the control of the English book trade while he was Bishop of London (1597–1604). In this period, the bishops of London and their chaplains were responsible for reading any texts thought likely to prove controversial and deciding whether they could be printed. Their role came particularly under the spotlight as Elizabeth I's long reign drew to a close, when speculation about the succession had created a political crisis. Shakespeare's account of Henry IV (1367–1413) was especially sensitive, as it justified the deposition of Richard II (1367–1400) by his successor, Henry Bolingbroke. The publication, in 1599, of Sir John Hayward's history of the life and reign of the same king had led to the imprisonment in the Tower of its author and of Bancroft's chaplain, Samuel Harsnett, who had licensed its printing.

These pamphlets seem to have been Bancroft's file copies, kept as evidence of the licensing process; no fewer than three of them bear the authenticating signatures of their respective publishers, Andrew Wise, Thomas Hayes and John Flasket, probably as proof that they had fulfilled their obligations to the authorities. Most notably, *The Second part of Henrie the fourth* has been signed by the bookseller Andrew Wise: this is the only known copy of any Shakespeare quarto to have been signed by the person responsible for seeing it into print.

Pauline and Catholic Epistles
Early 17th century, probably *c.*1604–1608
English; manuscript on paper, 332 x 215 mm
MS 98

THE PROJECT TO PRODUCE A REVISED TRANSLATION of the English Bible, commissioned by James I in 1604, was masterminded by Richard Bancroft, first as Bishop of London and then as Archbishop of Canterbury, although he did not live to see its publication in 1611.

Bancroft drafted instructions for the revisers, dividing them into six 'companies' based at Westminster, Oxford and Cambridge, each consisting of scholars fluent in the ancient languages of the Bible. The base text was the translation made in 1568 for the Bishops' Bible: 40 unbound copies of the most recent (1602) folio edition were distributed among the revisers, who compared this text with the other published English translations, drawing also on their own knowledge of the original texts. Revised versions were then circulated and a general meeting was convened at Stationers' Hall in 1609–10, at which the final draft translations were read aloud and discussed.

This manuscript is one of remarkably few surviving documents that shed light on this six-year process of revision by committee – a process that was ultimately (and perhaps surprisingly) successful. It contains draft translations of the Epistles of Saints Paul, James, Peter, John and Jude, prepared by the New Testament company at Westminster. Probably reflecting a relatively early stage in the process, it contains only about half of the revisions that were eventually published. The manuscript is ruled in red with two central columns and space for notes on either side. Although space was allocated for all the verses, it was left blank where the text of the Bishops' Bible was accepted without change. The right-hand column and margin are blank throughout, presumably to allow for further revision.

The Epistle of Paule the apostle to the Ephesians

The first chapter

1.

2. Grace be to you and peace from God our father and from the Lord Jesus Christ

3. Blessed be the God and father of our Lord Jesus Christ w[hi]ch hath blessed us w[i]th all spirituall blessings in heavenly places in Christ:

or, in Christ

4. According as he hath chosen us in him before the foundation of the world that we should be holy and w[i]thout blame before him in love.

5. Having predestinated us unto the adoption of children by Jesus Christ to himselfe according to the good pleasure of his will.

6.

7.

8.

9. Having made knowne unto us the mystery of his will, according to his good pleasure w[hi]ch he hath purposed in himselfe:

10. In the dispensation of the fulnes of times that he might gather together in one all things in Christ both w[hi]ch are in heaven and w[hi]ch are on earth, in him.

or, in the heavens

11. In whom also we have obtayned an inheritance, being predestinate according to the purpose of him who worketh all things after the counsell of his owne will.

12. That we should be to the prayse of his glory who first trusted in Christ.

or, hoped

13. In whom also ye have obtayned an inheritance, after that ye heard the word of truth, the gospell of our salvation: in whom also after that ye beleeved, ye were sealed w[i]th that holy spirite of promise.

14.

FINE BINDINGS AND DECORATED WRAPPERS

EDWARD CHALONER (1590/91–1625)

Sixe Sermons
London: William Stansby, 1623
English; printed text on paper, octavo
1623.12

JOHN DAY (c.1522–1584)

Certaine Godly Rules Concerning Christian Practice
London: T.W. for Thomas Knight, 1647
English; printed text on paper, octavo
G4500.D2 [**], acquired with the assistance of the Friends of Lambeth Palace Library, 1988

THE COLLECTIONS OF LAMBETH PALACE LIBRARY include many grand and elaborate bindings, either commissioned by wealthy owners or made for presentation to influential and important figures. Among these are bindings made for Elizabethan and Jacobean courtiers such as Sir Francis Bacon, Sir Christopher Hatton and Robert Dudley, Earl of Leicester. Among Archbishops of Canterbury, the most active patron of fine binding was probably Archbishop Matthew Parker, who established a bindery at Lambeth Palace and employed several immigrant French Huguenot binders.

On the evidence of the books preserved at Lambeth, however, the only archbishop who seems to have maintained a consistent aesthetic preference for the appearance of his library was George Abbot. Abbot's misfortune in killing a gamekeeper in a hunting accident in 1621 overshadowed his last 12 years as Archbishop of Canterbury. He withdrew to some extent from public life and may have consoled himself with buying books: many of these are bound in the same distinctive style, in limp parchment stamped with his arms in gold.

In the same period, but at the other end of the spectrum, the library also preserves an interesting and remarkably early example of a book issued by its publisher in cheap decorated wrappers. Very few copies now remain of John Day's *Certaine Godly Rules Concerning Christian Practice*, but it was a popular religious text that went through several editions. Copies of the 1634 and 1647 editions survive in wrappers decorated with woodcuts depicting biblical scenes.

Anno Dom.   MDCXXIX

Cæsar Walpoole Rector of St Thomas Apostle London gaue by Will 10ˡⁱ wherewith were bought these Bookes.

Mart: Lutheri Opera. tom 7. Witeb: 1582.
Mart: Chemnitÿ Harm: Euang: Franc: 1622.
  Eiusdem continuatio p̄ Io: Gerardū 1628.
  M. Chemnitÿ Exam: Concilÿ Trident: Gen: 1614.
  M. Chemnitÿ Lo: Com: Witeb: 1623.
Math: Flacÿ Clauis Scripturæ Bas: 1617.
  Math: Flacÿ Cat: Test: Veritatis Gen: 1618.

Abraham Colfe Rector of St Leonard Eastcheape London gaue 11ˡⁱ wherewith were bought these Bookes. 1.1.

Concilia Generalia. per Seuer: in: Binnium tom: 5. fol: Agrip: 1618.
Io: Caluini Opera. tom: viÿ. Vol. 9. ex edit: varÿs.

Thomas Wood B.D. Rector of St Michael Crooked Lane London gaue 10ˡⁱ wherewith were bought these Bookes. 1.1.1.

Hieron: Zanchÿ Opera tom: 3. Gen: 1619
Wolfgang: Musculi Opera. tom 8. Bas.
P. Martyr in Genesim. Lugd: 1606.
  Idem in lib: Iudicu̅ ibid: 1609
  Idem in Romanos ibid: 1613.
  Idem in Corinthios ibid: 1579.
  Loci Com: Gen: 1624.
  Idem in Samuelem Tigur: 1571.
  Idem in libros Regum Tigur: 1572.
Dan: Chamieri Controuersiæ Gen: 4 tom.

He gaue also these Bookes following. f.f.f.

Beda his historye of England Englished by J. Stapleton.
Fortresse of Fayth by Jo: Stapleton. Printed at Antwerp: 1576
The examination of Henry Iwitts and Iesuits in the Tower of London 1582.
The Execution of Iesuites and Priests for Trayson not for Religion. Printed at London 1583.
A Declaration of the causes mouing y Queene to aÿde the Lowe Countryes. Yere 1585.
A Discoverÿ of diuers Traysons agaynst Q. Elizabeth.
The Controuersÿes betwixt the Priests and Iesuites in England 3 volls.
Two Bookes in Latin of the same faction Rethempsions.
The Copyes of certayne discourses in excusing themselues.
An Answer to the Proclamation of K: Iames agaynst Papists.
The estate of English fugitiues vnder the King of Spayne. Printed at London 1595.

Henry Fetherstone Citizen and Stationor of London gaue. 1.

Twoo fayre Globes Cælestiall and Terrestriall. Printed at Amsterdam by Iansonius 1617.
A fayre Mappe of y whole world by Hondius Printed at Amsterdam by Iansonius.

Katharine Fetherstone his Wife gaue.

English Voyages. 4 Voll. by Sam: Purchas Printed at London. 1625.
Purchas Pilgrimage. at London 1626.

Henry Fetherstone gaue also these Bookes. 1.1.

America, siue, India Occidentalis descriptio accuratissima, vna cum nauigationum omniu̅ in partes illas relatione: Omnia figuris elegantissimis in æs incisis, et ad viuum expressis a Theodoro de Bry et eius filÿs. Francofurti 1586. Vol 3.

Asia, siue, India Orientalis descriptio. et quarundam Mapparum, locoru̅ maritimoru̅, vrbiu̅, Populoru̅, (veluti in India nauigatione versus Orientem suscepta, diligenter obseruata oræ) narratio. Omnia sedu̅ et diligenti industria in æs incisa, et ob oculos posita a Theodoro et Ioanne de Bry fratribus. Vol 3. fr̄nco: 1601.

Libri duo charactere Chinensi.
Officium B. Mariæ cum picturis. M.S.

Sion College Library
Book of Benefactors
1629–1982
English; manuscript on parchment, 450 × 350 mm
Sion L40.2/E64

Sion College Library
Register of Students
1652–93
Latin; manuscript on paper, 195 × 150 mm
Sion L40.2/E29

THE PRE-1850 COLLECTIONS OF SION COLLEGE LIBRARY, transferred to Lambeth Palace Library in 1996, provide one of the best-documented examples of the relationship between any early modern library and the community it served. Founded in 1628, Sion College was set up as a base for the clergy of the City of London, especially for preachers for whom no parish living was available. It provided both a social club and an intellectual underpinning for the London clergy, but its library quickly established a much wider reputation, both within the City and beyond.

The Benefactors' Book of Sion College Library records gifts of books, as well as money to buy books, from hundreds of Londoners during the first century of the college's existence. The donors range from aristocrats to clergy, from authors presenting their new book to bequests of whole libraries, from doctors and lawyers to schoolmasters and tradesmen, including many from the London book trade itself. The availability of some (albeit limited) resources to buy new books set Sion College Library apart from almost all other London libraries. From 1710, this was supplemented by the legal deposit privilege of being entitled to claim a copy of any new book registered at Stationers' Hall.

The extent of the library's ambition is evident from its printed catalogue of 1650, the work of John Spencer, Librarian from 1631 until his death in 1680. The first for any library in London, it was published in Latin, the language of international scholarship. The results may be judged from the library's admission register, which documents the arrival of readers from Oxford, Cambridge, northern Europe and the Baltic, and from as far away as New England.

ANNOTATED BOOKS FROM SION COLLEGE LIBRARY

Plato, *Omnia opera*
Basel: Johann Valderus, 1534
Greek and Latin; printed text on paper, folio
Sion Arc Quarto C11/P69

Peter Abelard, *Opera*
Paris: Nicolas Buon, 1616
Latin; printed text on paper, quarto
Sion Arc Octavo A46.3/AB1H

WORK TO DESCRIBE IN DETAIL more than 60,000 early printed books from Sion College Library has resulted in some notable discoveries and rediscoveries in recent years. Many of these books were already well used by the time they arrived at Sion College, either because they were gifts or bequests from their former owners, or because the college itself tried to eke out its resources by buying books second-hand. As a result, the Sion collections include volumes from some of the most interesting personal libraries to come onto the market during the seventeenth century.

The distinctive reading practices of the renaissance scholar, politician and diplomat Sir Thomas Smith (1513–1577) may be seen in his copy of the works of Plato (1534), which is annotated with carefully executed sketches to draw attention to passages in the text and to serve as aids to memory. This copy arrived at Sion College in 1712 as part of a very large bequest of books from the Church of England clergyman Edward Waple (1647–1712).

Many of the poems of John Donne (1572–1631) address the theme of compulsive love and its temptations. One book from Donne's library, bought by Sion College in 1643, contains the works of the medieval theologian Peter Abelard (1079–1142), including the celebrated correspondence with his pupil Heloise about their illicit love affair. Donne's tiny pencil marks in the margin indicate the sections that most interested him.

PETRI
ABAELARDI,
FILOSOFI ET THEOLOGI,
ABBATIS RUYENSIS,
ET
HELOISAE CONIUGIS EIUS,
PRIMÆ PARACLETENSIS ABBATISSÆ,
OPERA.

NVNC PRIMVM EDITA EX MMS. CODD. V. ILLVST.
FRANCISCI AMBOESII, Equitis, Regis in sanctiore
Consistorio Consiliarij, Baronis Chartræ, &c.

*Cum eiusdem Præfatione Apologetica, & Censura
Doctorum Parisiensium.*

PARISIIS,
Sumptibus NICOLAI BVON, via Iacobæa, sub signis
sancti Claudij, & Hominis Siluestris.
M. DCXVI.
CVM PRIVILEGIO REGIS.

Lambeth Faire:

Wherein you have all the Bishops Trinkets set to sale.

*I sit thus groveling in S. Peters Chaire,
Ore-prest with griefe to thinke on Lambeth Faire.*

These tricks and whimseys have been long conceal'd,
But now the pack's laid open, al's reveal'd.
The little *Patriarke* frets and fumes to heare
How cheap his knacks are sold in *Lambeth Faire*.
  You that delight in Popish ware,
  Come fit your selves in Lambeth Faire.

Printed in the Yeare, M. DC. XLI.

ARCHBISHOP LAUD AT LAMBETH

Lambeth Faire: Wherein you have all the Bishops Trinkets set to sale
London, 1641
English; printed text on paper; quarto
H5178.L2 [**], acquired with the assistance of the Friends of Lambeth Palace Library, 2016

IN MAY 1640, LAMBETH PALACE came under siege from a mob of London artisans and apprentices. The target of their anger was William Laud (1573–1645), Archbishop of Canterbury, who had escaped across the river to Whitehall earlier in the day, taking his silver plate with him. Later that year, Laud was impeached by the House of Commons on a charge of high treason, accused of supporting arbitrary government and influencing the king against his subjects, and by March 1641 he was a prisoner in the Tower.

Laud's intense unpopularity reflected deep suspicion of his promotion of church ritual and ceremony and the fear that his secret project was to re-establish the Roman Catholic religion in England. These were the themes of an extensive and highly personalised campaign against him in both manuscript and print. At least five different editions of *Lambeth Faire: Wherein you have all the Bishops Trinkets set to sale*, all published in 1641, mocked Laud and other bishops as defeated enemies, having to choose between 'Rome or Tyburn' and desperately trying to sell off their 'Popish garments', 'trinkets' and 'knacks' at Lambeth Fair. In this edition the title-page woodcut shows a group of churchmen, one with a speech bubble reading 'Time brings all to light'.

Many of Laud's possessions, books and papers were confiscated, but traces of his time at Lambeth Palace still survive. His expenditure to beautify the chapel, which retains its elaborately carved wooden screen, was condemned at his trial in 1644 as evidence of extravagance and popish sympathies. Like many seventeenth-century Englishmen, Laud was also fascinated by the exotic east. Another relic is the shell of his eastern Mediterranean tortoise, a trophy pet who outlasted his master and lived on in the garden at Lambeth for more than a century.

JOHN EVELYN'S BOOKS OF COMMON PRAYER

The Book of Common Prayer and administration of the Sacraments, and other Rites and Ceremonies of the Church of England
London: Robert Barker and the assignes of John Bill, 1639
English; printed text on paper, quarto
H5145.A4 1639 [**], acquired with the assistance of the Friends of Lambeth Palace Library and the B.H. Breslauer Foundation, 2015

The Booke of Common Prayer and administration of the Sacraments, and other Rites and Ceremonies of the Church of England
London: Robert Barker and the assignes of John Bill, 1632
English; printed text on paper, quarto
H5145.A4 1632 [**], acquired with the assistance of the Friends of Lambeth Palace Library, the V&A Museum Purchase Grant Fund, the Dulverton Trust and the Corporation of the Church House, 1977

THE BOOK OF COMMON PRAYER sets out the forms of service for worship in the Church of England at different times of the day, on special days of the year and for particular occasions. Lambeth Palace Library has exceptionally strong holdings, beginning with the first edition compiled by Archbishop Thomas Cranmer in 1549 and continuing with the subsequent revisions of the text and its many printings, in a wide variety of physical formats.

Among the most splendid of these are some volumes that once belonged to the seventeenth-century diarist and virtuoso John Evelyn (1620–1706). As a royalist, Evelyn spent much of the 1640s on the continent. While in Paris, in 1647, he married the daughter of Sir Richard Browne, the English resident at the French court for Charles I and Charles II in exile.

Paris was the most fashionable city in Europe and these years helped to form Evelyn's aesthetic taste and his fastidious collecting practices. It was also in Paris, in Sir Richard Browne's embassy chapel, that Church of England services maintained their visibility (as Evelyn noted in his diary), during a period when they were abolished in England. 'Your *Chappel*,' Evelyn wrote to his father-in-law, 'was the *Church of England* in her most *glorious estate*.' He later inherited Browne's handsomely bound copies of the 1632 Book of Common Prayer.

Evelyn's own copy of the 1639 edition of the Book of Common Prayer is bound in red goatskin, with his arms stamped in gold on the cover and his 'IE' monogram in all four corners. Evelyn seems to have thought this copy so beautiful that he kept it in a glass case.

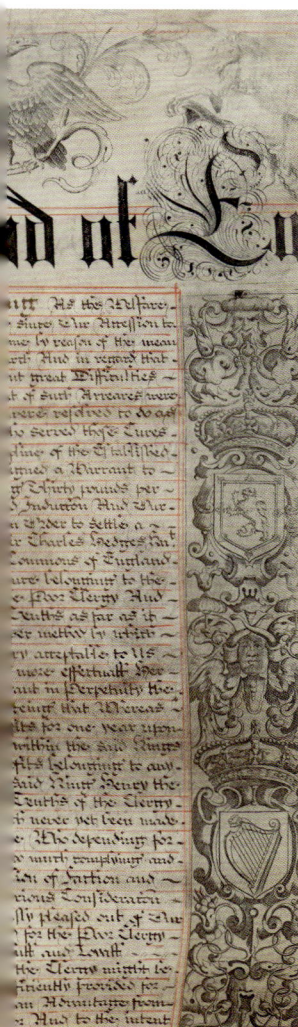

Queen Anne's Bounty Charter
The Governors of the Bounty of Queen Anne for the
Augmentation of the Maintenance of the Poor Clergy
3 November 1704
English; manuscript on parchment, 780 × 640 mm
QAB/1/1/1/1

AS THE ECONOMY OF ENGLAND CHANGED in the seventeenth and early eighteenth centuries, efforts were made to address inequalities of clergy income that derived from a system based on medieval land-ownership and patronage. By this charter of 3 November 1704, Queen Anne (1665–1714) set up an institution known as the Queen Anne's Bounty, granting it the revenue of 'First Fruits' and 'Tenths', taxes that had formerly been paid to the Pope and then (after the Reformation) to the Crown. This revenue was to be invested to provide for the livings of poor clergy, redistributing the income received from larger and wealthier benefices to make up the shortfall in funding smaller benefices.

Detailed information was collected about livings throughout the country, including those whose value was less than £80 per annum, their distances from London and whether their incumbents held more than one living. The records of the Queen Anne's Bounty provide much evidence about the level of clergy incomes and sources of income (such as farms), the physical repair of clergy accommodation, and the investments made on behalf of the Bounty, throughout the eighteenth and nineteenth centuries. Recent research by the Church Commissioners has confirmed that the Queen Anne's Bounty invested significant sums in the South Sea Company, which traded in enslaved people. It also received benefactions, many of which are likely to have come from individuals linked to, or who profited from, transatlantic chattel slavery.

In 1948, the Queen Anne's Bounty was amalgamated with the Ecclesiastical Commissioners to form the Church Commissioners for England. These voluminous records came to Lambeth Palace Library with the transfer of the Church of England Record Centre in 2020.

'FOUR INDIAN KINGS'

Letter from four Native American leaders, representatives of the Iroquoian Confederacy of the Mohawk River valley, to Thomas Tenison, Archbishop of Canterbury
Boston, New England, 21 July 1710
English; manuscript on paper, 310 x 195 mm
MS 711, f. 198

LAMBETH PALACE LIBRARY holds much material relating to missionary activity overseas. The first Archbishop of Canterbury to take an active interest in this was Thomas Tenison (1636–1715), who in 1701 helped to found the Society for the Propagation of the Gospel in Foreign Parts. The aim of the society was to raise funds to support the clergy in missionary work abroad, particularly in the rapidly developing American colonies.

In 1710 four Indigenous American representatives crossed the Atlantic to visit the court of Queen Anne in the hope of negotiating a military and political alliance against the French. Three were Mohawk chiefs from the Five Nations of the Iroquois Confederacy, while the other was a Mohican. 'The Four Indian Kings', as they were known, became celebrities in London, where they lodged in Covent Garden. They were granted audiences with the queen, who commissioned portraits of them for the royal collection. They were received by various other members of fashionable society, attended public entertainments, listened to sermons in church and visited the Tower of London and St Paul's Cathedral. When they came to Lambeth, Archbishop Tenison presented each of the chiefs with a Bible bound in red goatskin.

This evocative letter, written once they had returned home, thanks Archbishop Tenison and the Society for the Propagation of the Gospel for their kindness during their visit and for agreeing to send missionaries, 'to be Settled at a Fort with a Chappell', to counteract the influence of the French Jesuits. The letter gives both the native and English baptismal names of the chiefs, accompanied by drawings of their 'dodem' animals – a turtle, a bear and a wolf – indicating their clan affiliations.

May it please Yor Grace

We being God be thanked safely arrived upon our Native Continent can not forget Yor Grace and ye Society's favour and kindness to us when in Brittain and Yor kind promise of providing us wth Missionarys to be settled wth a Fort or a Chappell and house for them wch we pray Yor Grace and ye Society not to be forgetfull of

We pray that Anadagarjaux Col: Nicholson may find his Letter —

We are Yor Graces and ye Rt Honble Society

Boston in New England   Most Humble Servt
July ye 21st 1710

TWO LAMBETH LIBRARIANS

Andrea Soldi (c.1703–1771)

Portrait of Andrew Coltée Ducarel (1713–1785), c.1740

Oil on canvas, 1280 x 1000 mm
Presented by Lady Palmer, 2021

Reverend Samuel Roffey Maitland (1792–1866)

Sketches made during a tour of the Continent in 1828

Pencil, ink and watercolour on paper, 210 x 280 mm
MSS 1944

The lawyer and antiquary Andrew Coltée Ducarel was appointed Lambeth Librarian in 1757, despite his hopes for a more lucrative post at the British Museum. Over the next 28 years, Ducarel had a profound impact on the library through his work to set in order and describe the collections: the first published catalogue of the Lambeth manuscripts, which appeared in 1812, drew heavily on his labours. Ducarel also trawled intensively through the archives, producing many volumes of detailed indexes and extracts. His indexes to the archiepiscopal registers, from the thirteenth century onwards, comprise 67 volumes and are still useful. Some items from Ducarel's own correspondence and collections have found their way to Lambeth, vividly evoking his antiquarian interests and wide network of friends and correspondents.

The appointment of Samuel Roffey Maitland as Librarian in 1838 did much to make the Lambeth collections more widely known and more accessible to scholars. At his own expense, Maitland employed an assistant, enabling the library to be kept open on a daily basis for the first time. He also published, in 1843 and 1845, two pioneering handlists of the early printed books at Lambeth, identifying the continental books before 1520 and the English books before 1600. Unfortunately these innovations came to an abrupt halt in 1848 when the incoming Archbishop John Bird Sumner (1780–1862) appointed his own son-in-law in Maitland's place. As a young man, in 1828, Maitland had undertaken an extensive tour of France, Germany and Poland, which he described to his father in letters that are now at Lambeth, illustrated with lively sketches of architecture and local costume.

THE FIRST CHURCH IN AUSTRALIA

'Plan of a temporary place of Worship at Sydney, New South Wales', 1794

Ink and grey wash on paper, 397 × 531 mm
Papers of John Moore (1730–1805), Archbishop of Canterbury, vol. 1, f. 95

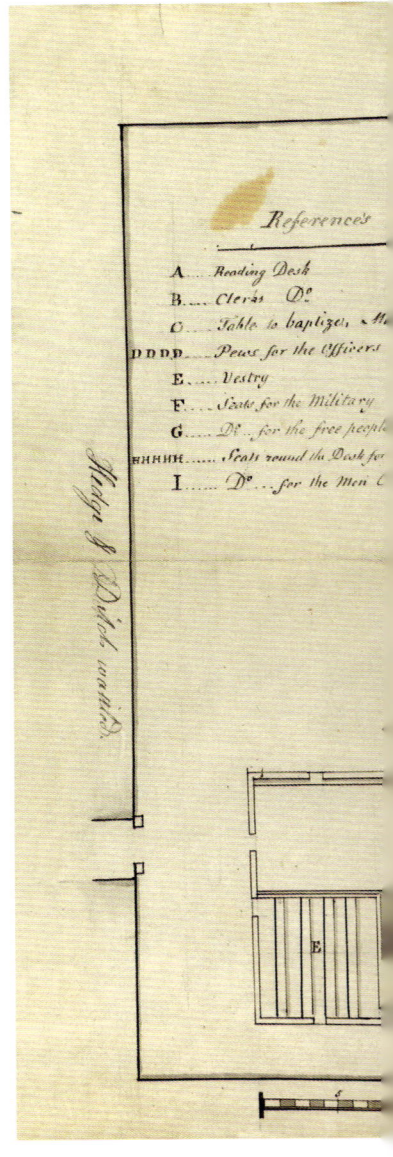

WRITING A REPORT BACK TO JOHN MOORE, Archbishop of Canterbury, Richard Johnson (1755–1827), the chaplain to the First Fleet – a group of 11 British ships that transported settlers to mainland Australia, marking the beginning of European colonisation – described the many difficulties he faced on arrival in Sydney Cove in 1788. He complained about the moral laxity of the colony, the drunkenness and debauchery of officers and soldiers, their lack of concern for the spiritual welfare of the convicts, and the tribulations and obstacles he encountered. He wrote despairingly: 'I declare that I cannot walk along the street or road, but I am almost sure to have my eyes and ears insulted with some wicked gesture, action or language.'

In particular, Johnson emphasised his frustration at the lack of a building for public worship in the colony and his conflict with Francis Grose, the Lieutenant Governor. After five years of conducting services, he complained: 'I stand out in the open air – when I have complained respecting the Heat, I have, with a laugh, been told that a Sentry Box was at my service.' At last, in March 1793, he set out to build a church single-handed and at his own expense: 'for days together I have myself been in the woods, stripped and working as hard as any Convict in the Colony.' Enclosed with his letters is a plan showing the wooden church at Port Jackson which he completed in August 1793 – the first church to be built in Australia. The simple plan depicts seating for some 500 people, with separate areas for the male and female convicts, soldiers, officers and free people.

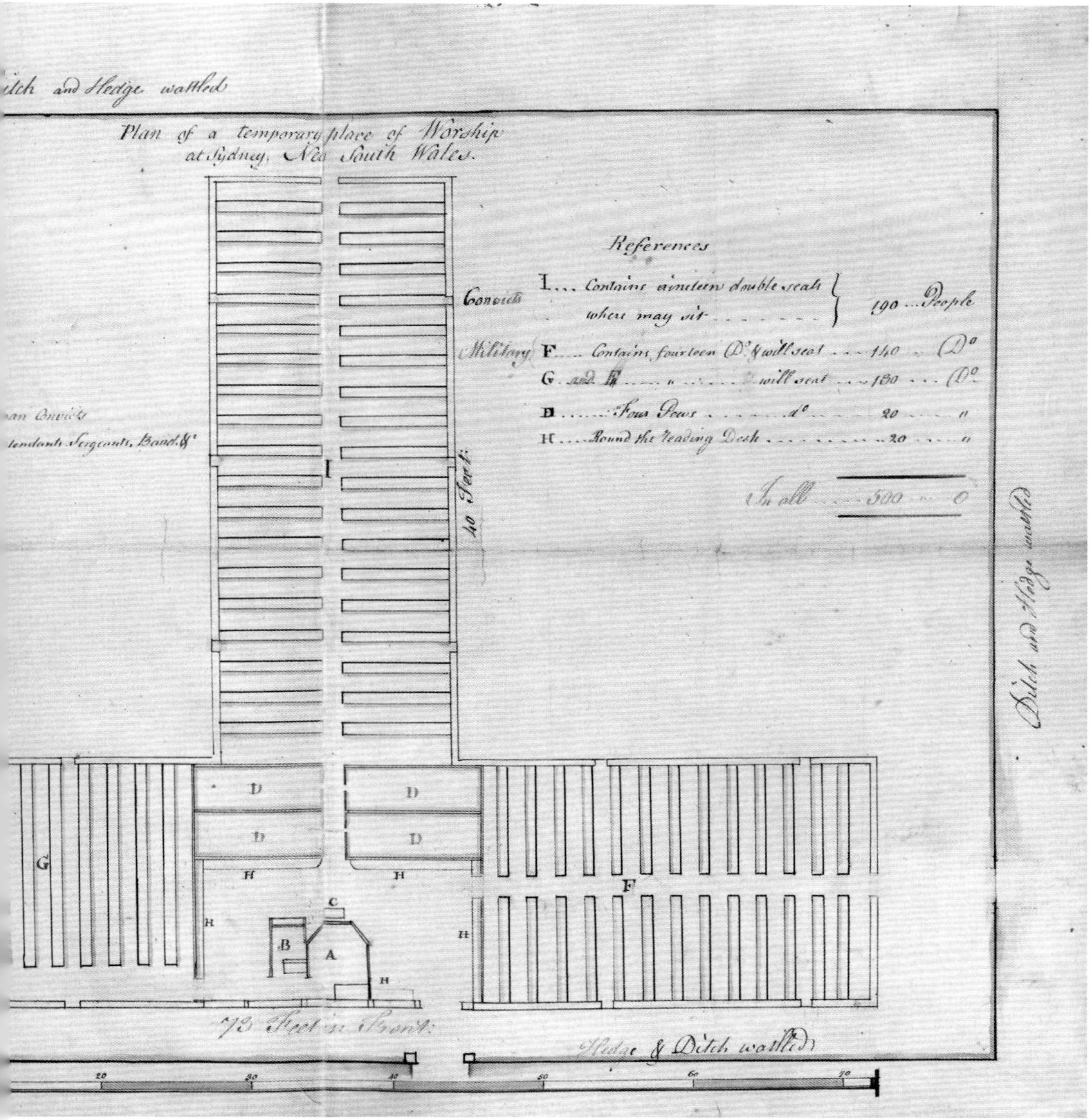

Plan of a temporary place of Worship
at Sydney, New South Wales.

References

Convicts I .... Contains nineteen double seats } 190 .... People
                where may sit

Military F .... Contains fourteen Do. & will seat ... 140 .... Do.
          G and E .... Do. will seat ... 130 .... Do.
          D .... Four Pews ... do ... 20 ...."
          H .... Round the reading Desk ... 20 ...."

                                In all ... 500 0

Ditch and Hedge wattled

73 Feet in Front.   Hedge & Ditch wattled

THE FIRST CHURCH IN AUSTRALIA | 71

The Queen cannot refuse Herself the pleasure of informing the Arch Bishop of the happy effects of His Visit to His Majesty. He expressed Himself to the Physicians after Your departure, satisfyed of the manner in which You had stated every thing to Him, to the Pages He said He was happy & to His other attendance, that He was thankfull. At the Visit this Morning He repeated the same to Her, with every possible expression of regard Towards the A. B. & was extreamly pleased with the Idea of seing Her & some of the Family this Evening.

The Queen feels much obliged to the A. B. for undertaking this unpleasant Task, which He has so delicately performed.

Charlotte

Windsor
the 10th March 1811

THE MADNESS OF GEORGE III

Letter from Queen Charlotte (1744–1818) to Archbishop Charles Manners-Sutton (1755–1828), 10 March 1811

English; manuscript on paper, 215 x 160 mm

MS 5164, acquired with the assistance of the Friends of Lambeth Palace Library, 2019

THE LAST TEN YEARS OF THE LIFE OF GEORGE III (1738–1820) were marred by prolonged and severe mental illness: the king's symptoms included sleeplessness, agitated behaviour and delusions. In 1811 a committee was set up, under the chairmanship of Archbishop Charles Manners-Sutton, to advise and assist Queen Charlotte in managing the care of her husband. This Queen's Council supervised every aspect of the king's medical treatment, requiring daily updates from the physicians and a quarterly assessment of his chances of recovery. One effect of this was to create an extraordinary archive (MSS 2107-2139) at Lambeth, in which no fewer than 3,075 of these reports are preserved, each numbered and dated by the archbishop.

The medical reports portray an 'irritable and violent' patient. George had come to believe that he was immortal, that southern England was sinking into the sea and that the Duke of Clarence would marry the Princess of Wales and sail off to Australia. For much of the time, the unfortunate king was restrained in a strait-jacket and sedated with opiates.

Archbishop Manners-Sutton played a key role in the delicate negotiations between Charlotte and her husband's doctors, whom she distrusted. In a letter dated 10 March 1811, the queen expressed her relief and gratitude to the archbishop and described George's positive reaction to the news, broken to him by Manners-Sutton, that he had been stripped of his royal powers in favour of his son, the Prince Regent and future George IV (1762–1830): 'The Queen feels much obliged to the A. B. for undertaking this unpleasant Task which He has so delicately performed.'

THE FIRST BLACK ANGLICAN BISHOP

Samuel Crowther, James Johnson, Henry Johnson and friends at the Wilberforce oak in Keston, Kent, in 1873

Photographic print on paper; 150 x 200 mm
Tait 219, f. 119

THE PHOTOGRAPH SHOWS A LANGUID SUMMER SCENE in the English countryside on 21 June 1873. In the centre, sitting at the foot of the tree, is Samuel Crowther (*c.*1809–1891), the first Black Anglican bishop, who had been consecrated as Bishop of Western Africa in Canterbury Cathedral in 1864. On the ground in front of him recline two other African clergymen of the Church Missionary Society: James Johnson (*c.*1836–1917), later Assistant Bishop of Western Equatorial Africa, and Henry Johnson (1840–1901), subsequently Archdeacon of the Upper Niger.

The moral charge of this image derives from its location, at 'the Wilberforce oak', at Keston in Kent (now part of Bromley). It was under this tree that William Wilberforce (1759–1833), the politician and philanthropist, is said to have resolved to announce to the House of Commons his intention to bring forward a motion for the abolition of the slave trade. This was commemorated by an inscription on a seat beneath the oak tree. The slave trade in the British Empire was eventually abolished in 1807 and the bill for the abolition of slavery itself was passed shortly before Wilberforce's death. As a boy, Samuel Crowther had himself been captured by nomadic raiders and enslaved, before being freed from a Portuguese ship by the Royal Navy. All three of his younger colleagues in the photograph were the children of formerly enslaved people.

This photograph and accompanying correspondence are to be found among the papers of Archbishop Archibald Campbell Tait (1811–1882). The Tait papers form part of the library's very full series of official papers and correspondence of the Archbishops of Canterbury, which begins in the mid-nineteenth century and continues to the present day.

'... With the shadows of evening gathering around him,
— alone and happy '...

The Reverend J.E.C. Welldon (1854–1937)

Gerald Eversley's Friendship: A Study in Real Life
London: Smith, Elder, & Co., 1895; second edition

English; printed text on paper, octavo; extra-illustrated in pencil, ink and watercolour on paper, 190 x 125 mm
Benson, BSN 12, acquired with other Benson family books, through the estate of the Revd K.S.P. McDowall and with the assistance of the Friends of Lambeth Palace Library, 2011

Since the Reformation, Lambeth Palace has been home to the families of many Archbishops of Canterbury, but the most extraordinary of these was the family of Edward White Benson (1829–1896). In 1859, while Headmaster of Wellington College, Benson married Mary Sedgwick (1842–1918). They had six children, of whom two, Martin and Nellie, died young. The other four all achieved distinction in their own right: Arthur Christopher Benson (1862–1925) as an academic and writer; Margaret Benson (1865–1916) as an Egyptologist; Edward Frederic Benson (1867–1940) as a prolific novelist; and Robert Hugh Benson (1871–1914) as a writer, preacher and Roman Catholic priest. The two youngest were still at school when their father became Archbishop of Canterbury in 1883. The family divided its time between Lambeth and Addington Park, the country house near Croydon that was particularly favoured by nineteenth-century archbishops.

None of the Benson children married, and in 2011 Lambeth Palace Library was able to acquire some 32 family books that had passed down through the descendants of Archbishop Benson's younger sister, Ada McDowall (1840–1882). Some are heavily annotated or extra-illustrated, and collectively they form a very lively record, sometimes poignant and sometimes hilarious, of the domestic life and intellectual formation of this immensely talented, but psychologically troubled family.

E.F. Benson's copy of *Gerald Eversley's Friendship*, a public school novel by J.E.C. Welldon, Headmaster of Harrow School and later Dean of Durham, has been interleaved and used as an album. It contains some 50 very lively cartoons in pencil, crayon, ink and watercolour, mostly by the three Benson brothers.

GUERNICA TELEGRAM

London/Canterbury, 27 April 1937

English; printed text on paper, 135 x 210 mm
Council on Foreign Relations: relations with Roman Catholics in Spain
CFR RC 211/3, ff. 26-27

THE COUNCIL ON FOREIGN RELATIONS (CFR) was set up in 1933 to take responsibility for promoting relations between the Church of England and foreign churches outside the Anglican Communion. It remained the Church's official channel for dealing with overseas churches until the creation, in 1970, of the General Synod's Board for Mission and Unity. The Council was finally wound up in 1981, when ecumenical relations were brought within the administration of Lambeth Palace.

The CFR files deal extensively with ecclesiastical relations, but they also offer a sidelong view of many important diplomatic and political matters, especially regarding wartime Europe, the British Mandate in Iraq, and relations with Communist Eastern Europe. High-level relations with the Papacy and the Ecumenical Patriarchate are another constant theme.

The Spanish Civil War (1936–39), in which the Spanish Catholic Church became deeply embroiled, was the first of the major conflicts of the twentieth century to be discussed in detail within the CFR papers. Archbishop Cosmo Lang (1864–1945) and his staff made cautious efforts to find out the truth behind the propaganda put out by both sides, whether it related to anti-clerical massacres perpetrated by the Republicans or the terror-bombing of civilians by the Nationalists. On 26 April 1937, the town of Guernica in the Spanish Basque Country was heavily bombed by German and Italian aircraft, at the request of the Spanish Nationalists led by General Franco (1892–1975). Some 1,600 civilians were killed and the town reduced to rubble, but Nationalist sources claimed that it had been burned by the Republican forces as they left. This telegram from a journalist broke the shocking news of the bombing in an attempt to elicit public condemnation from the archbishop.

This edition © B.T. Batsford Ltd., 2026

Text and illustrations
© Lambeth Palace Library 2026
Front flap; back cover; pp. 5, 12, 13, 14
© Hufton+Crow

First published in 2026 by
Scala Arts & Heritage Publishers Ltd
43 Great Ormond Street
London WC1N 3HZ
United Kingdom
www.scalapublishers.com
An imprint of B.T. Batsford Holdings Ltd.

In association with
Lambeth Palace Library
15 Lambeth Palace Road
London SE1 7JT

ISBN 978-1-78551-324-4

Project managed by Bethany Holmes
Designed by Linda Lundin
Printed in Turkey

10 9 8 7 6 5 4 3 2 1

Scala is represented in UK and Europe by Abrams & Chronicle Books, 1st Floor, 22–24 Ely Place, London, EC1N 6TE and 57 rue Gaston Tessier, 75166 Paris, France.

All rights reserved. No part of this book may be reproduced, stored in a retrieval system or transmitted in any form or by any means electronic, mechanical, photocopying, recording or otherwise, without the written permission of Lambeth Palace Library and Scala Arts & Heritage Publishers Ltd.

Every effort has been made to acknowledge correct copyright of images where applicable. Any errors or omissions are unintentional and should be notified to the Publisher, who will arrange for corrections to appear in any reprints.

Director's Choice® is a registered trademark of Scala Arts & Heritage Publishers Ltd.

FRONT COVER:
Detail from *The Lambeth Apocalypse*, c.1260–67 (pp. 22–23)

PAGES 2-3:
Detail from Wenceslaus Hollar, *The Prospect of London and Westminster Taken from Lambeth*, c.1707

BACK COVER:
Aerial view of Lambeth Palace Library, set in the Lambeth Palace garden, with St Thomas's Hospital and Westminster Bridge behind

POST OFFICE TELEGRAPHS.

53

RP + 155 1.53 LONDON @ 94

-RP 1/9 HIS GRACE THE ARCHBISHOP OF CANTERBURY

OLD PALACE CANTERBURY

= REUTERS SPECIAL CORRESPONDENT AT GUERNICA BASQUE ANCIENT CAPITAL REPORTS TODAY NUMEROUS GERMAN AEROPLANES IN FRANCOS SERVICE RAIDED CITY DROPPING COUNTLESS BOMBS HAND GRENADES SETTING WHOLE CITY ABLAZE CASUALTIES IMPOSSIBLE ESTIMATE BUT SAID TO BE HUNDREDS MEN WOMEN AND CHILDREN GUERNICA OF NO MILITARY SIGNIFICANCE ONLY ONE BARRACKS WHICH WAS BARELY TOUCHED WOULD GLADLY PUBLISH ANY EXPRESSION OF YOUR DISGUST AT SUCH WARFARE METHODS WHICH YOU THOUGH FIT TO SEND US BY TELEGRAM OR WILL SEND SPECIAL REPRESENTATIVE WAIT UPON YOU =

= EDITOR DAILY HERALD LONDON +